SUCCESS PLATFORMS

If you're starting a business or a business owner, *Success Platforms* is the must have book that you need to give you all of the business strategies to avoid the pitfalls and ensure the best opportunity for success.

—**Mike Filsaime**, CEO MikeFilsaime.com

Building a business is more than having a great product and putting a "For Sale" sign on it. *Success Platforms* provides the essential business manual that was just not out there before this. You need to add *Success Platforms* to your business toolkit.

—**John Thornhill**, 7 figure Internet Marketer, Planet SMS

As a CIO and professor, I have been teaching and counseling business students for over twenty years, I have often been approached by students and entrepreneurs who had brilliant ideas but no concept of how to develop and market their dreams. *Success Platforms* is the answer!

I have never seen an approach that makes the entrepreneurial process more simple and straightforward. What a seminal approach to the "impossible!" Make your dream possible by taking the journey using these understandable "truths!".

—**Lee Rizio**, Professor of Business,
UCSD Extension, ex-CIO for 20 years

Bryan Eaton has masterfully taken his many years of experience in various industries and used that to provide actionable instructions for anyone who is even thinking about starting their own business. There is a wealth of information in *Success Platforms* for anyone who wants to seize it and really make things happen"

—**Sean Wander**, CEO and Co-Founder Control Influence, LLC

SUCCESS
PLATFORMS

THE BREAKTHROUGH GUIDE
TO THE SUCCESS SECRETS OF
CORPORATIONS AND MILLIONAIRES

BRYAN EATON

NEW YORK

SUCCESS PLATFORMS

THE BREAKTHROUGH GUIDE TO THE SUCCESS SECRETS
OF CORPORATIONS AND MILLIONAIRES

Published in New York, New York, by Morgan James Publishing. Morgan James and The Entrepreneurial Publisher are trademarks of Morgan James, LLC. www.MorganJamesPublishing.com

The Morgan James Speakers Group can bring authors to your live event. For more information or to book an event visit The Morgan James Speakers Group at www.TheMorganJamesSpeakersGroup.com.

FREE eBook edition for your
existing eReader with purchase

_____

PRINT NAME ABOVE

For more information,
instructions, restrictions, and
to register your copy, go to
www.bitlit.ca/readers/register
or use your QR Reader to scan
the barcode:

ISBN 978-1-61448-500-1 paperback
ISBN 978-1-61448-501-8 eBook
Library of Congress Control Number:
2013930343

Cover Design by:
Rachel Lopez
www.r2cdesign.com

Interior Design by:
Bonnie Bushman
bonnie@caboodlegraphics.com

In an effort to support local communities, raise awareness and funds, Morgan James Publishing donates a percentage of all book sales for the life of each book to Habitat for Humanity Peninsula and Greater Williamsburg.

Get involved today, visit
www.MorganJamesBuilds.com

Habitat
for Humanity®
Peninsula and
Greater Williamsburg
Building Partner

To my wife, Natalie.
You are the most important
platform in my life.

CONTENTS

PREFACE

I want to thank you for purchasing and reading Success Platforms.

The seed that started this book came from sitting in a number of Author 101 University seminars held by Rick Frishman. It was here that I was flooded with a weekend's worth of seminars, speakers and training.

Over three days, in random order, various training, tools and techniques for getting a book to the public was presented an hour at a time. At the end of my first Author 101, I was a bit confused. Five months later, I attended the Author 101 seminars a second time. Again, it was three days of information that came in random order and left me sorting out the order of execution for them. It became clear that there were a series of subjects that needed to be mastered to be successful in the book industry. In fact, these are the same techniques that I had mastered in business over my multiple careers in media, technology and advertising.

My professional career started as a radio station Music Director in San Francisco. I had been the recipient of the record label promotion efforts. I even had some friends who were record company promotion men. I also had a background in retail sales, advertising and public relations. As part of my need to pay the bills as a radio announcer, I had a second job as an audio visual expert at one of the top ten conference hotels in the United States. I was a computer systems designer and programmer. I am currently a certified project manager. I have successfully managed multiple million dollar programs to completion. There have also been some that did not succeed. After many decades, I have seen what works and what doesn't at a hands on level.

It became clear to me that anyone wanting to author a book successfully needed to have more skills than adequate writing.

Authors wanted to be published. To be published they need an agent to get a publishing deal. Getting an agent required that you had a platform. The size of this loyal following of readers would serve as a customer base that would be pitched to the publisher as core of your book's audience. A first time author usually won't have an audience. So, it feels like a self defeating circle.

From this, Success Platforms was born as the guide to achieving success in whatever you endeavor to do. It became more than just how to successfully author, publish and sell a book. With my various backgrounds and careers, I had experienced successful and some not so successful ventures. It is really true that there are lessons in your mistakes. There is also guidance in the things that worked well.

Success Platforms condenses many decades of business and personal experience into the elements of success. Building each as a platform of its own focuses on the many areas that success requires. Understanding and ascending each is key to building the foundation to success. As each platform is completed, they combine into the platform that gives up success.

There is a great amount of focus on making money or making millions. While making large sums of money is a great motivating force, it is not an end in itself. If you achieve millions and lose your health, you are not in a position to enjoy the benefits of that money. Some people achieve wealth with only achieving more wealth as their reward.

I have achieved many successes in my life. My goals were rarely a million dollars. My experiences have been many and each has taught me something. I have made mistakes as well. When I was in radio, I saw a few artists become millionaires and stars. I also saw that they lost some privacy and some of their ability to have personal interaction. Over the years, some of these very same artists lost as much as they made. They learned from their mistakes and reinvented their careers. Some drifted away from the spotlight.

Mistakes are part of life. There are parts of my past I would like to redo. There are parts I would not change even though they had a cost to them. Today, I am a very different person than I was in my mid-twenties. Some mistakes change us because they are do or die decisions. I had a few of those. Some things about me are less drastically changed. People and relationships change and yet they leave traces on who we are. There are many to whom I owe thanks and many to whom I owe apologies.

The coffee cup in front of me has a quote from Abraham Lincoln on it. "The best thing about the future is that it comes one day at a time." This is true of success as well. Take each day and do the best with it that you can. I have had days where I have made an effort to reach out and apologize to those in my past. There are days when the list of things to do exceeds my stamina to complete them. There are days when I reach goals. Life is never the same day to day.

New opportunities and people present themselves in our lives. It becomes important that our learned lessons are applied to current situations. Even to the extent that apologies to people in our past are in order if we get an opportunity.

Abraham Lincoln is said to have failed at most of his jobs. I contest that idea. He simply took jobs that allowed him to read. It was his reading that educated Lincoln. Each of his jobs was social. They allowed Lincoln to be known and liked by entire towns. There is much to be said for likeability. In fact, Lincoln became president not because he was everyone's first choice; but, because he was everyone's second choice. As I said, there is much in favor of likeability.

Sometimes we need to be aware of our surroundings and the lessons they direct us to. As I was waiting to record an interview with literary agent, Bruce Barbour in Los Angeles, I was suddenly facing an attractive woman. She had approached me and now sat next to my chair. She asked if she could ask me some questions about how she could be successful. Now, remember, I had not fully created Success Platforms at this point. It reminded me of the many times as a teenager that my peers turned to me for counsel and advice. It seems the universe is saying I need to be there for people seeking guidance and counseling.

This book has a definite business slant and approach. Nonetheless, as I wrote each part, I kept asking if each part had personal applications. Most of it does.

Find your goals. If the guidance to build a platform for your goal seems indirect, think about what could change to make it apply. The techniques are there. Sometimes they just need to be modified to fit each situation.

To find additional comments and information that supplements the book here is always the website for the book, check the Success Platforms website at www.successplatforms.com.

ACKNOWLEDGMENTS

I want to thank all those who have touched my life in all ways and placed me on the path I find myself today.

Thanks to everyone at Morgan James, especially David, Scott, Rick and Robbi for your belief, support and guidance. Bethany and Margo for getting this into a deadline.

Bryan Jr., with unconditional love, my thanks for sharing your earliest years with me. Thank you to my Mom and Dad, brothers, Scott, Bill and Gary, and my sister, Lee Anne. To my nephew, Dr. Joe Eaton for our chats on book writing and his support. To Ron R. for mentoring me and sharing radio success as few get to. Buzz and Ardele, thanks for the many years of support, friendship and being there.

To Bruce Schindler, Bruno Menezes, Ed and Muriel Wilcox, my thanks for your many years of friendship. To the many Author

101 University alumni, who provide support and guidance each time we meet, my thanks.

The biggest thank you to my wife, Natalie, for all her love, support and guidance. There are not enough words to express the joy, love and support you have brought to my life.

Finally, to my readers, I wish you all the best as you build your Success Platforms.

INTRODUCTION

Success Platforms is written as both an instructional book and a series of exercises that are designed to focus you in achieving your goals.

There is a huge amount of information available to anyone building a successful enterprise. Distractions can come from every angle as you get bombarded with various coaches and courses that claim to give you the answer to making millions. In the end, most of it is rarely new. Success Platforms is built upon experience. Not just my personal experience, but the experience of most corporations.

One secret that most corporations won't share is that they are regularly losing the tools that make them succeed. Those tools are the workers who make their business.

People leave jobs for many reasons. Regularly people reach retirement age and leave a company. They take with them the special knowledge accumulated over the time they worked at the company. Some people leave because they find better jobs. Usually they have less knowledge about how the business runs. This represents a loss of talent potential that may or may not be replaced by a company. As more and more companies choose contractors as the bulk of their labor force, the knowledge of those workers is an expected temporary acquisition. Documentation and structured processes keep the knowledge within the corporation.

Success Platforms builds and documents your knowledge base. The twelve platforms are individual areas of expertise that must be successfully achieved. They are not completely independent of each other. They are also not completely integrated.

Your Mind Platform is designed to clarify your goals and vision. This is your first platform and is your starting point. It builds a basis for all the other platform work.

Your Expert Platform helps you define the area of expertise that you will use in creating your success.

Your Financial Platform identifies the basic financial knowledge you will need to succeed at anything.

Your Product Platform identifies your products and the path they take in reaching a customer. A well defined product strategy supports an easier sales path.

The Strategy Platform addresses areas of risk and issue discovery. It also looks at the impact of communication on success.

The Selling Platform addresses the sales flow process and the integration of a product line into it.

Your Publicity Platform addresses the building of your audience. With the introduction of the Internet, opportunities for building a customer base have grown. Your Publicity

Platform looks at today's marketing world and your options for getting found.

Your Mentoring Platform looks at the importance of having a mentor. The difference between coaching and mentoring is explained.

The Activity Platform addresses the planning of activities in reaching your success. Each stage of activity planning is addressed.

The Online Platform looks at the importance of the Internet and social media. Internet marketing resources play an important part in building a customer base.

The Performance Platform introduces metrics and formulas for determining how successful your marketing and sales activities are.

Your Success Platform looks at general success information that crosses all platforms.

You should have a notebook dedicated to Success Platforms. Each chapter includes exercises that should be performed by you. By keeping all the information in a single notebook, you can see your growth through the Success Platforms program. If an exercise is a daily one, you may want to have a second notebook for those exercises.

Thanks again for being part of Success Platforms. I encourage you to sign up to the mailing list at www.whatisaplatform.com or scan the code below.

The Success Platforms book you are reading will be updated from time to time and becoming part of the Success Platforms mailing list will keep you up to date. Also, this will update you on any examples or additional exercises that expand this book in the future. You may also visit http://www.successplatforms.com for all relevant information to Success Platforms.

Chapter 1

YOUR
MIND
PLATFORM

People want to succeed. Businesses and individuals spend a huge amount of time, energy and research to make sure they succeed. Whether you are starting a venture or need to revive your current one, you can assure your success by using the same techniques that businesses use.

In Success Platforms, those practices and procedures are synthesized into each platform's building blocks for success. Most concepts of platforms are focused on a single activity or topic. In software development, the platform is the operating system or design framework used to build the applications. The publishing field uses platform to describe the reach and appeal of the author. A platform can be generically defined as a support structure upon which an elevated activity can take place.

Success Platforms expands the platform concept to consider multiple platforms as the components of any successful activity.

The degree of an activity's success is dependent on the success of all the component platforms. The weakest link of the component platforms poses the most risk to your success.

Business activities are defined by programs and projects. Programs are the ongoing activities that run day-to-day within a business. Within a program, there are many projects. It is important to understand this distinction because it can help in your ability to understand the scope of every task you plan. Projects are those activities that have a specific goal and a specific end. Any activity that has an end date and a goal can run like a project.

For everyone with glowing ideas of making the next big success, not all businesses succeed. In fact, very few people can just open a storefront and have a product that is instantly accepted. It takes coordinated planning and strategizing along with a lot of work to make a business succeed. It also takes an understanding of businesses and how they function to get your business moving towards that goal line.

A survey of businesses showed that of all the projects started by businesses, roughly seventy-five percent failed.[1] Obviously, businesses that failed on most of their projects would not survive. There had to be a change. Businesses determined that well-defined planning and implementation activities were keys to a higher success rate. Once businesses identified specific processes for the planning and implementation of projects, the numbers changed in favor of bringing in projects successfully and within budget. The adoption of clear project processes reversed the failure percentage.

---

1   CIO analysis: Why 37 percent of projects fail, By Michael Krigsman for IT Project Failures, March 15, 2011, http://www.zdnet.com/blog/projectfailures/cio-analysis-why-37-percent-of-projects-fail/12565

A clear project process, or methodology, created a success platform for businesses.

I have a secret I want to share with you. You are a business. Everything you do is a business. Even your personal life is a business. You need to understand and implement processes to reach each success whether a business or an individual. Approach everything as a project where you want to succeed.

Success is achieved a step at a time. The successful completion of each step raises the chances for a successful project. Reaching each stage raises the project to the next platform towards its success. A successful platform takes into account all the methodologies for success within each stage of your work. It identifies the task, risks and benchmarks that need to be met to reach goals.

Platforms

Potential publishers want to know about an author's platform. They want to know about your potential audience that already likes your writing. Also, they want to know how much influence you have on them for purchasing your book. It seemed odd to call it a platform to me initially. I mean, come on, why a platform?

A platform in this sense is focusing on only one stage of the book publishing or product sales process. That makes sense for a publisher trying to understand the market demand for a book. One will have to achieve success in many platforms to be totally successful.

There are two basic questions. What is a platform, and why should I have one?

Imagine yourself in a crowd of people. Everyone starts shouting his or her message. You start shouting your message. Soon there is a loud roar of noise that makes no sense.

If you are in a crowd and start speaking, are you heard better than if you were standing on a stage? You are not. If you do some required things, like go up a few steps to a stage, you can be seen and heard better than if you were in the crowd. By standing on a stage, you are able to rise above the crowd and be heard. Those in the crowd, without the platform, are more likely to stop focusing on their message and listen to yours.

How does a platform foster your success? By taking certain steps, you arrive at a level above the others. Stepping on a platform we have a better opportunity to promote and share success. It allows us to influence more people in a way that moves them to share and consume what you are presenting.

The television program "Star Trek"™ showed Gene Roddenberry's idea of where man and technology would be in the centuries ahead.[2] In fact, the television show was so well portrayed that the government wanted phasers and tricorders from the production company. They had to be told that these were just props. They did not really do all those things. Yet, today, we see in our cell phones and tablet computers a world very close to Roddenberry's imaginings. In fact, many of our advances in technology were born in the minds of young inventors who had been influenced by science fiction like Star Trek.

Everything we do or wish to do is going to come from our minds. We have a vision which is the highest perception of what we want. It is that vision which gives us the other activities and platforms that need to be successfully achieved to make our vision real. We are all capable of taking the steps, if we know what they are. Understanding each platform and the incremental steps that

---

2   Star Trek ™ & © 2011 CBS Studios Inc. All rights reserved. STAR TREK and related marks are trademarks of CBS Studios Inc.

need to be successfully completed within each platform are the blueprints to success.

The very first platform is the Mind Platform. Everything starts with an idea. We must be able to be able to have an idea before we can make anything real. Things that never existed came into being because an individual imagined them. Ideas are the seeds that grow into successful business or personal ventures.

Before you can influence people, you must have something to share. The most important element to your success is an idea that is uniquely yours. Because we are all individuals and have something unique to share, we can use our experience and knowledge to achieve success. You are unique because of your experiences. Your personality, delivery and perspective combine to take your message and deliver it your way. Develop products with your personality and viewpoint.

A product is any item that you can make and can be sold. Products can be as simple as a short electronic document on a subject or as complex as a manufactured product. It has to provide value to your customers. They have to be willing to buy it.

In the last fifty years, we have had a tsunami of new technology. In the 1960s, there were few credit cards and no debit cards. We used checks and money to buy things. Today, we are moving towards electronic currency. I can transfer money using my phone or computer. You see the transfer arrive in your bank account by a message to your phone.

Three decades ago, the personal computer used a text based operating system. Today, our computers are increasingly smaller and more natural to the way we interact using voice and action commands. It's been a tremendous transformation which started with ideas.

To be able to start anything, you have to understand what you are trying to achieve. Your ideas need to be expanded and validated. Your path and what is to be your success needs to be understood before you begin.

Understand your vision deeply. You should be able to close your eyes and see yourself in that vision. Be able to write your vision down. Be so intimate with your vision that you can answer questions about your vision as if it were fully realized today. See your vision completed.

Before he was famous, the actor, Jim Carrey, wrote himself a ten million dollar check as a reminder of his vision. Later, as he became more successful, he had more than that amount in assets. The writing of the check was one way to make his vision more real.

The mere fact of imagining something does not guarantee success. What makes the difference between an idea and a success is the platform on which it is built.

What Do I Want?

What will you need to build your Mind Platform? You need to be able to know what you want. You need to have ideas that you review and adjust until they clearly state what you want. As you make them clearer, you will understand the idea(s) that will become your vision.

Quite often the beginnings of our quest for success start as one general thing that is not well defined. As the ideas are refined they become better understood. Sometimes, the initial ideas are not our final ideas. They are the seed of your success.

This first step identifies your vision or charter and what you believe. Determining our beliefs is critical to our success. Write them down. Revisit them as often as possible. Keep your focus

Exercise: Focus Your Goals

I'll be giving you a number of exercises to work through in each chapter. I highly recommend you have a notebook that is only used on your success platforms.

- Spend at least 20 minutes in the morning and evening writing down what you want.
- In the morning, write down the top ten things you want in your life. It's okay if you want to write down more than ten.
- In the evening write down your top ten goals again and write down five things you've done to support achieving your goals and five things you've done during your day that did not support achieving your goals.
- At the end of the six weeks, look at your original goals and the goals at the end of 6 weeks. Identify how your goals may or may not have changed.
- List the top ten things you've done in the last six weeks that support your goals and the top ten things you've done that do not support your goals.

This personal exercise will guide you to see how your goals and actions either support or sink your success over time.

on what you want. If any of your behavior is working against getting what you want, you will be able to see that and change those behaviors.

A charter may be a new concept to you. In business, a charter is written to legitimize project work. It identifies the reason for doing a project. A charter will describe at a high level the tasks that will be performed. It will define what makes the project a success.

Every project starts with a charter. Charters validate the process of getting what you want. They answer basic questions. What defines my success? Where and when will I start? What will I do? Who will be involved? A charter is developed to identify the purpose of the project activity.

In business, the person asking for the project to be done and the person(s) responsible for completing the work both sign the document. This identifies the main people who started the activity and why it is done.

In a personal setting, your charter will identify what you want to achieve as a goal. Your goals will be the detail of your charter.

The basic 5Ws used in journalism are who, what, when, where and why. You will also need to answer how.

In journalism, they break down a story into its components. You will need to break down your vision using the same process. Writing the answer to these questions kicks off the beginning of getting what you want.

Develop a charter or vision to describe what you truly want. Believe it. Do whatever you need to achieve your success.

A charter should be able to identify what you expect. It should clearly identify what can be expected at the end of the project and what will have been done to consider the effort as a success. The clearer it is the better. This will keep you focused on your definition of success. It keeps your activities on target.

Your charter will include a description of your vision. Once, you understand your vision, your dedication to

Exercise: Charter

Write the answer to the 5W questions:

- What defines my success or goal?
- Why am I doing this?
- When and where will I start the process?
- Who will be involved?
- How will I get there?

Write your charter in your notebook using the answers to your questions. Use no more than 5-6 sentences. Once you are satisfied with your charter, write it on something that can hang on your wall. Your charter should be visible by you often. This might be a good reason to buy a whiteboard.

making that vision a reality is the next step to address as you rise up the platform. The level of success you achieve will be equal to the level of commitment you make towards achieving your vision. It is the dedication to successfully completing each step that will control your success or failure.

It should be fully crafted in your mind. Mentally define and clarify your goals. This will help you complete your mind platform successfully.

In short, your vision must be fully understood by you. It must be able to be described by you. It must be made as real now in your ideas as you want it to be in your real life later.

When we look at what we desire and our vision, how many of our desires need to occur to have our vision. Those are our

Exercise: Write Your Vision

- Write down ten (or more) things you want in your life. Your list should be detailed. If any item in the list can be made specific, you should continue to revise the list until there are no more details you can add.

- Continue to move each to a more general idea until you can't take it further. These are likely the elements of your vision.

- Take your notebook and write your vision. Make sure it is the broadest expression of what you see as your vision. Include yourself in the vision.

goals. Goals are the incremental things we want that support our vision or charter. Each goal is a "mini-vision". They are the smaller successes we must achieve to be able to hold our larger vision as a success.

Add to your notebook any additional goals you think you need to achieve to support your vision. There is no limit. There is no right or wrong at this point.

FEAR and Conquering the Mind Platform

One of the biggest obstacles to getting what we want is FEAR. We all have experienced not getting what we want. We know what disappointment feels like. That apprehension can even prevent us from taking first steps to getting what we want. Like in the Wizard of Oz, Dorothy could always have gone home. It wasn't until she had the adventures that she acquired the experience that allowed her to believe she could go home. You need to be able to click your ruby slippers and have your goals. Just like Dorothy, you can always go home. You just have to ask.

The awareness that you can have your goals now is a large part of achieving success. If you have doubts, your negative beliefs can get in the way of your success. Let's expose fear for what it is.

FEAR is an acronym for False Expectations Appearing Real. Think about how situations involving fear play out. At first, we are apprehensive and maybe even picture some negative outcome. As we proceed into the activities that we need to perform, the negative expectations we anticipated either don't occur or are far less difficult than we thought. Those things we thought were limiting us have disappeared. They were false expectations that didn't exist and for some time appeared like reality.

If you were to enter a dark room at night, you might experience fear. Were there reasons that prompted your looking into the room? Maybe you heard sounds? Well, those reasons are issues that prompted your actions. The noises aren't creating fear. They are creating caution. You then act accordingly. On the other hand, as kids we sometimes fear the dark. Yet, when the lights are turned on there's nothing there. This is a clear example of FEAR being False Expectations Appearing Real.

Your perspective and your beliefs are very important. If you are a negative person or are surrounded by negative people, it's much harder to achieve your goals and your vision. It is clear that a vision is needed to be able to succeed.

Your belief needs to be so deep that it becomes real to you. You should be able to visualize each result as a success. Keep your positive focus on what you want. Keep your vision and goals written down where you can see them. Spending time in the morning and evening with your goals and vision is a great habit to acquire. You must have patience.

It takes about six weeks to implement a change in your life. Six weeks from today, if you set your mind to a visualized goal and follow the required activities to achieve it, you will be different. Your perception determines your credibility level about anything. Choose to look at everything in the most credible and supporting way. Nothing is impossible. The late actress, Audrey Hepburn, is credited with the quote "Nothing is impossible, the word itself says 'I'm possible'!"

Think of the vision as the ultimate definition of what your success is. The path to define and achieve your vision requires positive thought. A clear and positive vision is the right track.

Your Charter is your Mission Statement. Some corporations have their Mission Statement on the wall of their lobby. They reinforce that charter by repeating it in everything they do. These are steps you can take to realign your perspective.

Create a list of affirmations that clearly identify what achieving success looks, feels and smells like. If you exercise or run, repeat them during your workout. In time, you will retrain your mind to embrace your vision.

It is critical that you reach a point where the shift in achieving what you want becomes a natural part of your person. You'll find the negative people in your life either transformed or missing. You will be an uplifting, positive person. Your influence will affect others and affect your goals.

Right now you are focusing on what you want, but the ability to visualize your success as real is your advantage. Sometimes the power of thought requires that you take yourself out of your routine. Find a spot where you can go to think. When you focus your thoughts, you often come away with insights and different directions. If you can see the new insights as if they were already in place, they are likely strong tools for you to use.

Use your time to be able to experience your goals and visions as if they were achieved. What will it feel like? What does a normal day look like? Do your goals and vision have a smell? How will you feel? How will others feel and act?

Have you ever woken from a dream that was so real you weren't sure you were dreaming? The dream did not have substance and wasn't real in your waking life. Yet, dreams like this are vivid and real as we experience them. Get your mind to envision what you want to this same degree. If what you want is real to you now, it easily will present itself in your life.

Fear of failure is a subtle force that can creep up in you as you build your Mind Platform. Sometimes it can present itself as a paralysis. Sometimes, it can show up as things you do that don't support getting what you want. It may be as simple as having people in your life who limit or control your vision. These people may even be strong influences on you. They may be focusing on what makes you fail rather than what can make you succeed. Keep focused on success by the choices you make. Always align with success. Choose actions that have successful endings. You will see your goals.

Being positive does not mean blindly saying "yes" to everything. It is important to be realistic about your goals and vision. We all change. Your vision will change. Your goals will change. Evaluating your vision and each goal for its validity and likelihood for success is what helps us maintain our positive approach. Take each goal and ask questions about it. Throw out those goals that aren't likely to succeed. Remove any goal that might have a negative consequence. Success is hard enough. Keep a positive attitude.

Build good support mechanisms around your vision and goals. Have an inner circle of people with similar goals who get together to discuss each other's visions and goals. Act as a support group for each other. Find a mentor or coach who can add an extra pair of eyes to what you want to do. Make sure that what you want is a realistic goal. Once you have goals defined, you can help yourself succeed. Be positive. You can support your positive viewpoint by making sure you don't have surprises along the way to your success.

Since things rarely go smoothly, risks and issues need to be identified. Skillfully crafted resolutions to potential problems should be identified before you get into the thick of the process. You can't just make it up as you go.

Success requires understanding your message. Have a clear idea of what you will do and what determines your success. There are also potential pitfalls in the journey to achieving your success. Sometimes the goal changes and often what you are working to achieve based on your original idea changes as the journey unfolds.

A friend of mine once was at a self-help seminar. One of the attendees insisted he was a failure. He had always been a failure and did not see any possible way of changing his life. As a process of changing his path, he was asked to give a lecture on failure. After all, he was apparently an expert on failing. They set the time for that evening. He announced the lecture to the people attending the seminar a few times during the day's activities.

The next day, he reported back to the attendees that no one had attended his lecture the night before. Indeed he had failed.

The leader of the seminar stopped the man and asked him why he thought that he had failed. "Well, no one showed up", he said. The seminar leader pointed out that he had succeeded. There is no greater success that can you get from a lecture on failure than to have it utterly fail.

There are lessons in failure. It is how we envision and work with those lessons that refine how we can create success. Do not be afraid to fail.

I mentioned that having a support group is one of the support systems you want in your toolbox. Many voices speaking in unison will create an incredible force for your good.

Many years ago, I was working three jobs while trying to get a job working as a radio announcer. One day, I was working as an audio-visual technician for a positive thought seminar at Asilomar in Monterey, California. I mentioned to one of the speakers that I had submitted an application for my dream announcing job. He brought together the remaining ten to fifteen people in the room and had us join hands while in a circle. He had everyone affirm in one voice that I would get the job. Within the next week, I received a call that I had been chosen for that job.

I have since tried to make sure that every successful goal I seek has a strong support group behind it affirming the success I want in one voice. It illustrates the point that you need a clear vision and a clear voice supporting you. Then, you will find the world in alignment to your successes.

Successful building of any platform is a result of taking input activities and action, performing specific activities using those inputs. Then, outputs are created from successfully completing the activities in question.

In project management circles, this is the essential definition of the process that is repeated within every phase of a project

To this point, the Mind Platform has included identifying our goals and vision. Once you have identified them, write your vision and goals down in your notebook.

The expression of ideas into written words has power. Write a charter that gives the outline of your goal, your activities for achieving that goal and what defines your success.

Everything in your world sprang from some idea by someone. This is pretty strong evidence that ideas are powerful. Your success is formed from ideas. It is the effort that you put in to make it real in your mind that will determine whether you rise above others. Do this and you can complete a platform that serves as a strong foundation for your success.

Be Positive. How you approach everything will have an influence on how successful you are. Just to focus on the concept of positivity may seem like a difficult task. If you find yourself blocked at any point, get out your notebook. Write down the items blocking you. Show how you support them with your normal activities and how you help them.

A support group will be your strongest ally in achieving your goals. Have an open expression within the group that your goals and vision are real. This moves you closer to success. Affirm that what you want is real. These positive statements by your group will move you further to making it real. Visualize your result as real.

Your perception defines your belief of the world. It is your choice about how you want to perceive it.

In the 1920's, salesmen travelled the many country dirt roads in autos, like the Model T. Typically, the dirt roads had deep and narrow ditches at each side to drain off water. If a Model T tire ended up in a ditch it was stuck. The tall and narrow tires kept the car from getting out without some major help.

During one rainy night, a salesman found himself in just such a situation. His car was hopelessly stuck in the ditch on the side of the road. In the distance, he saw a farmhouse with a light on in one window. He started walking towards it telling himself that people in the farm areas were very helpful. He would probably be out of the ditch that night with the farmer's help.

As he walked, he thought of many things that might prevent him from being helped. What if the farmer had a bad day and refused him? Maybe he was a cranky type. Maybe he would turn him away to sleep in his car. Maybe his wife and he had a fight. Now, he was not going to help some interfering stranger. With each step, a new hypothesis for why he was not going to be helped entered his mind.

The salesman found himself suddenly at the front door of the farmhouse. He stepped on the porch and knocked on the door. More lights came on. The farmer came to the door. As the farmer started to say hello, the salesman abruptly shouted at the farmer; "That's fine then, don't help me. I wouldn't have wanted your help anyway with that attitude." The salesman stomped off to sleep in his car during the rain.

In the story, the salesman actually talked himself out of the opportunity to get the help he was seeking.

All too often, we can alter our perceptions to believe the opposite of the reality. Alternately, we can align our perceptions to be the new reality we want. You have the power to make the realities you want.

Finally, you need to determine what success is for you. If each platform is a component to our achieving success, we must have a clear picture of that success. Then, climb each platform to make it real.

Chapter 2

YOUR EXPERT PLATFORM

One result of Success Platforms is that you stand out. By the successful completion of the specific processes to complete your goals, you will stand out. Your success will define you. It makes you an expert.

Expertise is often reinforced by some form of acknowledgement of your skill in a particular area. Some people have college degrees to show they are expert in their field. Some people enter contests and win trophies. There are certifications that verify expert knowledge through testing.

Sometimes expertise comes from other experiences. Think of experiences you've had that gave you knowledge in something else. You may have undiscovered skills. Think outside the box. Discover what you know that you picked up along the way. It may be something that defines your expert skills.

When I was young, my older brother appointed me as his personal back scratcher. As much as I disliked the position, the experience exposed me to a wealth of Top 40 radio from Chicago. I grew up on the rock and roll radio of WLS in Chicago. There were also many hours of suffering through Chicago Cubs baseball games. My perspective, at the time, was that I did not want to scratch his back. I wanted to get outdoors and play.

The experience of listening to all that radio was giving me new skills. The knowledge of all those songs gave me the skills to become a Music Director in San Francisco. I grew up on the early Top 40 rock and roll heyday. It was my expertise in knowing the music of a generation before me that allowed me to excel at creating a radio sound. That station with its mix of oldies and adult contemporary music, along with sports broadcasts, was a successful combination. It brought listeners and sales. The success was further acknowledged when the radio station was awarded the Billboard Magazine Station of the Year award.

Opportunity – An Input To Your Success

I mention the Billboard award because the story around it identifies how opportunity provides the opening door to being successful. It was late summer. My boss was on vacation. I read in Billboard Magazine that the submissions for Radio Station of the Year were being taken. The deadline for submission was in two days.

This was the situation. I was seen as a crazy music guy by many of the management team. I wanted to submit the station for an award. It was the industry leader, Billboard magazine. My idea faced some initial objection. Against the resistance of the promotion department and my annoying urging, the written submission was approved and sent off in the mail.

Two things were critical to this experience. One was the opportunity. In this case, my discovery of the open submission was the opportunity. I can honestly tell you that my mind was saying, "We can win this!" I could sense it as if it were actually true right then. Of course, when there was resistance (and possibly office politics), it put in danger what I knew to be true. I persisted. I argued for at least opening the door to the next step. I think it was begrudgingly considered not so bad an idea. From that point, every member of top management took credit for the discovery.

Expertise

One thing that you can do to show that you have expertise is to get a certification. Certifications can come in the form of diplomas or trade certifications. Almost everything has certification for its correct execution. Certification is an acknowledgement of fluency in any area.

One of my neighbors told me that his son had become a vice president of a major technical firm in Silicon Valley and he did not hold a college degree. He had taken courses with certifications on almost every technical area he could.

I hold a professional certification in project management. My certification has made me a member of a group who qualify as an expert in that field. Employers acknowledge the certification as a mark of my competency as a project manager. As part of certification, there is testing against a common set of knowledge that reflects your mastery of the subject matter.

Education and experience give you expertise. Degrees in your field show that you have spent years studying your area of expertise.

What is your area of expertise? If you don't have an obvious answer, then you have yet to climb the Expert Platform.

Exercise: What Am I An Expert In?

Get your notebook.

- Write down all your interests. Include any of your hobbies in the list of your interests.
- Write down all the jobs you've had.
- Does any of your experience in or outside of employment give you expertise?
- To the right of each item, rank it from 1 to 10 with 10 being the highest or best response level and 1 the worst.
- Rank each for the highest level of knowledge and experience you have in each.
- Mark the 3 where you know more about the subject. Write down the people you know from each subject matter. Which item has the most people?
- What could you do to prove you have expertise in each one?

Think Success

As you've written down your areas of experience with, how many are successes for you? It is likely you have identified successes that are different from each other.

Not every success is defined by the same values or goals. Achieving the values we prize is often the mark of the traits that worked for us. They are the experiences that combine our hopes, thoughts and dreams around that activity.

As mentioned in chapter one, your perspective determines your experience. It is the concept of a glass half empty or a glass half full. It is about how you look at it. Sometimes how you present something to yourself makes all the difference. If you always work to think for the positive and success, you'll be ahead of those that don't.

The first step to success is to know when you see an opportunity. The next step is to act on it.

In the Billboard Magazine story, the opportunity was initially resisted because of who presented it. Later, the opportunity was acted on because it was presented as a potential success. It helps to have a good product. In this case, a potential win would improve the business of the radio station. When we won, it showed how many people with the same intention improve the odds for success. It also helped that we had a great product.

Communication

Communication is another input to creating an expert. Without communication, you may be an expert but no one will know. If you cannot communicate the terms of what makes a success, you are never going to have a goal to tell you when you have succeeded. A website is one communication channel that explains about you and about your product. I communicate my personal blog information at http://www.bryaneaton.com and deliver information specific to success platforms at it's own website (http://www.successplatforms.com).

By now, you should have some idea of a few of your talents. Do you have proof? It is the common acceptance of your proof of

Exercise: Five Areas Of Expert Knowledge

- In your notebook, write five ways you can prove that you have expertise in the areas you wrote down as your expert areas.

- Where you can't get five proofs of your expert knowledge in an area, brainstorm on ways you can add to your proof of expertise.

expertise that gets you to success. You can always create a test case as an example of achieving a goal. Documenting the steps and successes of your test case or cases can go a long way to proving your success.

In some cases, a sign of success is the amount of money one receives for following the process. In others, money may not be the primary criteria of success. Money will be a component of your success most of the time.

Retooling

Sometimes retooling and reeducating oneself is the key to expertise. If you find that you just don't feel expert enough in anything, then learn something new and learn it to the best of your ability. The ability to show that you really know what you are doing is critical.

Define your success factor. If you know what you are expert at, identify everything that would be an impressive display of your expertise. Use this to develop your presentation of your expert knowledge to others. It's very hard to argue with success. Once you have this down you'll be able to craft how you communicate your expert status.

The World's Foremost Expert On ...

Be careful about what your claim is. I was attending a seminar and one woman was asking many questions. Before each question, she would tell her name and announce that she was the world's foremost expert on relationships. As she spoke, it became clear that the claim of expertise was more hype than fact. Her questions showed she was far from being expert.

On my way home, I sat next to another attendee of the seminar. The woman came up in our conversation. In the audience, there were a number of psychologists. They had been working on a book on relationships for many years. The woman claiming to be the world's foremost authority had no credibility with the psychologists. She was not the world's foremost authority. Unfortunately, she had made the claim in a room with true experts on relationships. As a result of a false claim, she lost credibility.

The point is that expertise requires proof and credibility. You can't just proclaim yourself an expert.

Standing Out From the Crowd

Once you are an expert at something you need to expand on it. Scholars write papers and articles that are published in journals. Their peers then acknowledge them. Their work is more than idle chatter.

Write your book. A published author can always point to the published document that identifies the sum of their knowledge. Identify a problem that your expertise solves and address that problem in every way you can.

The model for standing out has changed in the last decade and will continue to change. Making a video and posting it to

You Tube or writing a blog are as important as writing papers for publication. It is important to know your stuff and also to share it.

Elevator Speech

It is crucial that you be able to tell what you are expert at. One of the best ways to make your point is to have an elevator speech and a follow on speech. The elevator speech is the concept of being able to have something that defines your expertise in a few sentences. Here is the concept. If you were to have an elevator ride with one person who could make your goals into a success, what would you say in the few seconds you have?

When making an elevator speech, identify your expertise and why you are an expert. Were any articles or books published on the subject? Are there test cases? Have you made a lot of moneybased on your efforts? In just a few sentences, you should be able to hit all the impressive points about you and your expert knowledge.

You should be able to raise questions in your listener's mind from your elevator speech. In fact, you should be able to

Exercise: Finding Your Expertise

In your notebook, answer the following questions:

- What am I expert at?
- What problem does my product or expertise solve?
- What training or certification do I have?
- What successes have I or others experienced following my expert guidance?
- Have you achieved either a direct or indirect monetary benefit that provides a level of success?

anticipate the questions and have answers already prepared. Any good elevator speech will provoke drill down. You will prepare your elevator speech in detail in the Activity Platform.

Assume for the moment, that you are selling your services in your area of expertise. Let's say that you are selling your expert service at one million dollars. If you were the buyer, what would you want to know from an expert for one million dollars? Using this premise, you should be able to identify a number of questions that should be asked.

These are your talking points for the follow on discussions. Your questions can be objections to buying the service. The questions may be clarifications on statements. You should be able to talk about the details of test cases and published works. Be prepared to show how your services saved someone money or made money.

In my test cases, I always try to monetize the results from specific trainings or exercises. As one test case was working on goals, he accomplished a long list of tasks that he had been putting off. If he had hired people to complete the tasks, he would have paid $10,000. That number puts some measurement on one exercise. Being able to put a value on your expertise tells others that you are the expert.

Be able to duplicate your results. An expert knows the subject matter without effort. The steps to success in the expertise should be identifiable and measureable.

A standard disclosure is that the results discussed are normal or not normal. Since there is never a guarantee that repeatable methods will always be wildly successful, be reasonable about what you claim.

Be able to back up why you claim to have this expertise. Finally, communicate. Communicate clearly and often. Help others succeed in your area. Volunteer your services to prove your expert knowledge. Show how you have solved a problem more than once. Nothing succeeds like success. Make some successes for your platform.

Chapter 3

YOUR FINANCIAL PLATFORM

A t some point money will be part of your success. We've looked at the mind and your expertise. I know you're starting to feel enthused about where this can go. The late Zig Ziglar, the sales expert and author is attributed with defining a sale as the transfer of enthusiasm from one person to another. Your enthusiasm is part of your expert platform.

You are ready to transfer your enthusiasm. You are ready to get out there and start working on your success. Not so fast. The reality of success is that it also requires that a good understanding of money and finances.

One of the first things you will discover is that starting and making a business successful costs money. It also requires good analysis skills. At a personal level, you need to make sure your income meets or exceeds your obligations. The ability to plan your financial expectations keeps you on course.

A business model is a description of how your business operates. It defines your business process. The good thing about a business model is that there are very few new business models. Most business models that fail are not around anymore. You benefit by being able to study existing models and use them in your efforts. Finding out why businesses fail helps you avoid problem areas.

If you have a credit card or a bank account, you get a statement every month. The statement shows what you spent and how much money remains in your account. Every month, you know where you stand financially. You can plan your financial life for the coming months. In addition, we all share a common requirement to pay taxes.

Accounting seems to be a term that strikes fear in people. Maybe because it seems very complicated we resist learning about it. The basic concept for accounting is not so hard. On one side money comes in and on the other side money goes out. The key is in understanding how to manage what goes on in between.

You should be familiar with a few basic items used in accounting. Now you might be asking why you need to know this. After all, you can just hire an accountant to handle all this.

In the 1940's and 1950's, the singer, Doris Day, made her fortune from movies and record albums. By the late 1960s, she was almost bankrupt because her accountant did not handle her finances correctly. She finally won a judgment in court against him, but millions of dollars were lost for good. This is why you need to be able to have enough knowledge about finances to protect what you earn.

Work Flow and Accounting

Accounting can also help you understand where you are in reaching your goals. Without proper accounting, you may have to abandon your efforts. Even goals unrelated to making or spending money will require accounting. You may need to make some money to stay afloat.

There are two kinds of accounting systems, double and single entry. Every accounting system uses a basic ledger to monitor the money moving around in your accounting.

A double entry accounting system will show all the money coming in (credits) on one side of the ledger entry and all the money going out on the other side of the ledger. In a double entry accounting system, the General Ledger is the main record of the business transactions. At the end of the month, the entries in the General Ledger must true up. The total money in must equal the money that went out plus the money you have on hand. Every amount in or out will have an account. Some usual double entry accounts include current assets, revenue and expense items, fixed assets, liabilities, gains and losses.

A single entry accounting system puts all entries in the same list or column. Money going out is represented as a subtraction of that amount from a running balance that is calculated after each payment. You can tell the amount of money you have at a glance.

Chart of Accounts

One of the first things you will need to do in any accounting system is to identify a Chart of Accounts (COA). This is a list of areas where you spend money or get money. You or your accountant will create this in your accounting system. This organizes your finances into categories. From your Chart of

Accounts you can get a snapshot of your financial health based on the information they contain.

There are seven basic categories in which all accounts are grouped:

- Assets (physical property owned by the organization)
- Liabilities (debts you owe)
- Owners equity (the amount left for the owner's after all the liabilities are paid)
- Revenue (the money that comes in)
- Expense (the money you have to pay out)
- Gains (Any increase in value from something purchased, like a stock or a piece of property)
- Losses (Any loss in value for something that was purchased)

A chart of accounts has a few main headings that categorize the accounting detail. These are usually identified by a numbering system for each main heading. There will be accounts that are specific to each company or person or each general accounting heading. If you pay or receive money from them, they will have a unique account. These will have a number assigned to them. The first numbers of the account will identify their main chart of accounts group.

I know this is technical, and you may not find this terribly exciting. Financial knowledge is your key to knowing what you have and what you owe. I recommend taking courses in accounting or educating yourself from books and online.

What I do want to cover for you are the types of information you can get out of your accounting system and how they can influence your success.

Projections and Budgets

Financial success requires planning. You have to identify the roadmap you are expecting to follow to reach your end point.

Let me share a secret, you are probably not the first person to do your type of business. There are equivalent businesses out there. Research your equivalent businesses. There are statistics that identify specific information about those businesses. You can find the average financial information for the business type. Find the equivalent business comparisons to see if you are on the right track. Your ability to succeed is built on your understanding of your business and its potential. You should be able to create an example of your business type on paper. You should be able to identify an estimated income, estimated cost of doing business and an estimate of how much profit you should have at the end of a year. If you like how it looks on paper, you probably have a good business idea.

It's OK To Have a Loss

Businesses don't open their doors and immediately become profitable. It often takes a few years to build a business into a success. Your customers need to know you are here and selling your product. You need to show them why you are different. Once you build a good customer relationship, your business will improve. When Amazon.com first started, and for many years afterwards, it ran at a loss. To build its business, Amazon offered free shipping on every order to gain customers. In their business model, they planned for the loss and made sure they had enough money to continue to run until they could start showing a profit. Amazon, as of this writing, is a primary supplier of books and other products online.

Sales Are Everything

As an entrepreneur, you are always representing your product and making matches between you, your product and your customers. It is a numbers game. There is some ratio of the number of attempts to sell something against the actual making of the sale that can effectively tell you what your work effort is. This conversion of the attempts to a successful sale can also help you understand your hourly cost of getting a sale.

This is only one of the items that can help you identify how much effort you are putting into each function of your business. There is also a dollar amount that you can place on these activities. Find that dollar amount and you now have a number or metric that you can use. Use business research to see if you are within the average for businesses like yours. Learn the percentages that are typical for all your business expenses. Apply that to project what you will likely spend as you do your business day to day.

Financial Planning

It is hard to get where you are going if you don't have a roadmap. Your financial roadmap should be made early and reviewed often. In fact, if you ever need financing to support your business you will be making these reports.

Budget and Profit & Loss Statement

You should be working to a budget. Make a list of the major areas of your accounting, both income and expense and break it down by each month. Once you know how much it will cost to be in business, you will know how much you need to sell to break even and to make a profit. Project your business out five years. You will know what your business path should look like. It will also give you an ongoing opportunity to update your budget based on how your business grows or changes.

You also need to make a profit and loss statement. A profit and loss statement reduces your five year budget down to the bare minimum. You can see where your expenses are against your income. You will have your business health in a single view.

Educate yourself about accounting and taxes or have an expert to guide you. Certain activities and expenses are deductions to your taxes and are needed to offset earnings for the tax calculation. A good accountant can help identify tax deductible expenses that will increase your profit and reduce taxes.

Invest To Grow

Sometimes you just have to spend money. Planned expenses benefit your business or tax situation. This is not wasting money. Planned expenses are a necessary part of you getting ahead. You do not want unplanned expenses. That is why you make a budget. You should know what you have today and what you expect to have in the future. You cannot just wing it. If you think you can, you need to change how you think about money and business.

Expect to make the following reports as you build your business or personal success:

- *Sales estimate*
- *18 month profit and loss*
- *Profit & Loss statements*
- *5 year plan (Budgets and Profit / Loss statements)*
- *COGS (Cost Of Goods Sold reports*
- *Percentages of spend & Income versus the average for your business type.*

Rinse and Repeat

Every month make sure you update your financials. Your budget should be updated with actual information. Actual sales and expenditures should be added to your budget. Every month see if you're on track.

Don't expect everything to be exact. You should be able to perform to within some variance of your projections. Say you are using ten percent as your variance, if you are twenty percent off, you need to do your budget projections again based on the twenty percent difference. Then, strategize about the things you can do to get back to a ten percent variance.

Remember, finances, money and numbers are your friend in anything you do. You must spend as much time on the financial end of your business as you do on the other parts. If you don't, you won't be able to steer your business to profitability and success. It might even result in a surprise when you find that you have less in the asset column than you expect. Financial change can happen very quickly and affect what you do at very deep levels.

There is a show on television where billionaires host potential candidates for angel funding on their products. The billionaires are referred to as sharks. They make no bones about the fact that their number one interest is making more money. There are steps that the person presenting her or his product goes through in the presentation. They get funded based on their potential and ability to make money.

The Financial Platform moves you through the process of defining what you sell, the price and the process you will follow.

Up to this point the platforms have been focused on you or your business looking inward. Now, this platform develops what and how you or your business will present its expertise to your consumer.

Chapter 4

YOUR PRODUCT PLATFORM

Every platform has inputs to a process. The process generates an output that either stands alone or feeds into another process.

One of the inputs to the product platform is the list of items that you are expert at. Also, in the list are the experiences that led to having the expert knowledge.

A product platform process is defining all the possible items that you can create from your expertise that other people will desire. Another process is the creation of a profile of your successful customer. A successful customer is a person, persons or business that you want to accept your success product on the terms that you have defined.

As a result, one output will be more decisions about what qualifies as your success. Another output will be a profile of your consumer.

Exercise: Prioritize Goals

- In your notebook, write down your desires that would be your ultimate goals.
- Next to each one. List it's priority from one to ten (one being the highest, two the next highest and so on)
- Describe each goal. Create something that would show it was already achieved. If it is selling products, then write the invoice. If it is making millions of dollars, complete the check.
- Put the item where you will see it at least once a day or more. Every time you see it think about the success you have.

What are the terms you want to get for your expertise? Initially, there are ideal goals. Sure, it is often not realistic. Yet, it is from that ideal that we define realistic goals and success.

Do you remember the check Jim Carrey wrote to himself? When he wrote it, some might have said it was out of reach. Writing the check clearly defined his goal and how it looked. It defined his success.

It is important to create a representation of that ultimate success. Even if it is only a written paragraph, the definition of the uppermost goal in your life needs to be done.

Sales are a common part of reaching success. Yet, there must be something to sell. We must be able to turn our expertise into something tangible. Your product should also be in demand. The more demand the better.

A number of years ago, I decided I needed to supplement my income. I sold healthcare products part-time. One of the items was a bath gel. At the time, most people used the standard soap bars and the idea of a gel in a bottle for taking a shower was outside what most people expected. As a result, the demand was not there. Now, after years of advertising barrage, the idea of a bath gel is a common thing.

If your product is accepted by people, it is likely to be successful.

People need certain things to survive. People like certain things because they feel good. Some products are bought because they are popular. People either have one or want one.

The Pet Rock˚ was one of those items everyone had to have. It struck a chord with almost everyone. When I was working in advertising, our creative director had developed the pet rock packaging. He felt his greatest contribution to the project was to force the price of the novelty item at twenty dollars. The perceived value of a pet rock was kept high because of the price. Not everyone was going to be able to get a real pet rock for a small amount of money. It created an impression of exclusiveness. It was also fun.

Exercise: Viral Characteristics

- In your notebook, draw a vertical line down the page. On the left side, write down a list of viral items. It can be anything from a video online to a consumer product like a portable music file player.
- On the right side, write down what makes them viral. What basic need do they fulfill for those that have them.
- Use this list as an input to your product development. Try to make sure your products fulfill as many of these characteristics as possible.

This sounds like something going viral. It represented many people's desires. Fun, exclusivity, value and required ownership all make up viral demand. Strive to design everything with as many viral components as possible.

Define Your Consumer

When I first got my job in radio, I was working with one of my best friends. I vividly remember our first discussion about the format we would develop for the station. I asked who the target markets were and was told women 18-35 and secondly, men and women aged 25-49.

I performed a high level analysis of what happens from high school to graduation. In high school, there is a media-frenzied identification with peers. Then, depending on her path, she either goes to college with a reduction of peer identity or to a mother at home with a peer group consisting

Exercise: Target Definition

- In your notebook, write down the answers to the following:
- Who is your target market? How big is it?
- Because you want to find the broadest market available, take the largest target markets you have and write them down.
- Write down what you think they are like. What do they need and what do they desire? What types of things do they buy and why?
- Use this list as an input to your product development. Try to make sure your products fulfill as many of these characteristics as possible.

of herself and her children. Her peer identification is reduced over time.

We had interns cut articles from magazines. They highlighted the basic points with a marker. The on-air personalities read these in between the music. It took off and soon the on-air staff was giving recipes for cooking fish in the dishwasher to their listeners. The format grew virally from the basic premise.

Develop a customer profile. Who will use your product? How old are they? What type of house do they live in? Do they rent or own their home? What is most important to them?

You are defining a fictional customer who needs what you are selling. When you are done you should have a profile with hobbies, physical status, income level and a list of problems that your average customer wants to solve. You will know what they need and what they crave. What will they buy at a discount? What will they buy at any cost?

Some things are consistently consumed by people. Food, clothing, housing and all the other necessities are constants of life. Some items fulfill basic human needs to feel good and be accepted.

Validate your previous assumptions with some numbers. Find statistics to back up your assumptions about your product. What is the financial make up of this market?

Many of the internet marketers will call this a *niche*. They use the many analytical tools from Google and others to determine what people are searching at any given time. They can tell the size of searching base and the geographic location of potential customers.

There is a saying that a shift in delivery systems causes a shift in the marketplace. As shopping and product delivery becomes more electronic, the use of online tools and survey results add to the understanding of your consumer.

Understand what makes an individual desire something and you can position your product better for purchase. Remember your enthusiasm has to transfer to your buyer. Your product must be presented with that enthusiasm. It is not enough to tell your customer that it solves a problem. You must tell them that it is the best or how it satisfies their needs like no other.

The Sales Platform Funnel

A sales funnel describes the products you have to sell and can include the process of reaching your customers with each offer. Selling is a numbers game. Only a percentage of the people approached will buy a product. To succeed you have to reach out to many people. If you have determined that ten percent of everyone approached will buy your product, then ten out of every one hundred approaches will result in a sale. This ten percent is a conversion rate. You are converting your potential customer into a customer.

You can convert your current customers into buying more items or more expensive items. The concept being that if they have opened their wallets once, they are likely to continue.

Imagine everyone who buys your product all together in one room. Not everyone makes the same income. Each person will have a different definition of what is expensive.

Someone making six figures could find parting with one thousand dollars for a product as something worth considering if it fulfilled a need. Someone making seven figures a year would be more open to purchasing a product with less concern for need fulfillment. The price will reflect both an ability to pay and a perception of need. Because a purchase will depend on the

conversion rate of the offer as well as the perceived need and value of the product, you should have multiple levels of product at varying price ranges.

Divide an estimated percentage of your customers into various income ranges. Create products based on your research that those customers should buy. Mold the products to address varying needs that would be addressed.

As your products become more popular, adjust your price accordingly. Do not undervalue your products. Aside from setting a value on the product, price adds a perceived value for the customer. As in the pet rock story, the perceived value based on the price did more to give the humble rock value than if it

Exercise: Funnel

- Develop your own sales funnel.
- Use the diagram in this chapter and within each segment put the product and price.
- List the expected income range of your customer for the product
- List the expected need or problem the product solves.
- List the features that make this the best solution available for solving this problem.

had been less expensive. If your product includes your time, as you become more successful and more popular, your time should increase in cost.

When you need to come up with a product and need guidance on your option, there are a number of potential products that can be developed based on your knowledge. One option is to write a book or a series of articles on your subject matter. You have the option of following a traditional paper publishing model or using the internet to deliver electronic versions of them.

If you want to create training materials in your area of expertise, you could develop a training program on CD or DVD. Your trainings could also be delivered electronically. Webinars provide the ability to bring your customers together for training in real time.

If you find material created by someone else that you want to sell, you could become an affiliate and receive a commission on each sale. Working with other marketers in a joint venture situation, or JV, you can leverage the mailing list of other marketers to promote your product for a fee or commission.

As your list grows, your site can be segmented into free and paid sections. For a monthly membership fee, you provide access to your private site pages and provide valuable extra material for your members. Finally, you can create a conference where paid attendees get training and guidance from yourself as the expert and/or multiple guest speakers.

Upsales and Downsales

You should always take full advantage of every sales opportunity. If you offer free information on your first customer encounter, take the opportunity to offer something related to your free information that they see as a must-have product. A tool or a report with critical advice that solves a customer problem should be offered after giving the free product. This is called an upsale.

Not everyone will take you up on your offer. For those that do not, give them an opportunity to purchase a different item with reduced features. This downsale opportunity should be presented as a reduced solution to their problem. Be clear about what it lacks and why you can offer it at a lower price. You may possibly indicate that the offer is missing an item that cost you thousands of hours to make. It shows a true value but without the high overhead of the costlier element.

Be careful not to have your upsale and downsale items be seen as the same offer at different prices because of the placement in the sales cycle. Make sure they are clearly different products.

Product Reviews

Your products and sales funnel should be a visible model of the products and expected conversion rates. As you develop marketing strategies and start selling, continue to refine your sales funnel. Because nothing is constant, you should consistently review and update each of your platforms regularly. Base your review on the results of each strategy you use. Set an expectation of the effort involved to achieve success. If something is not working well, change it. If something works, use it consistently.

If your goal is to make large sums of money, you may have multiple sales funnels. You may even have sales funnels within sales funnels depending on how your marketing and sales strategy is designed. Sometimes, a strategy will require new products. It may even call for products within products. Success takes effort and commitment.

Chapter 5

THE STRATEGY PLATFORM

Almost every successful activity or venture includes other people. To have others involved in your success requires communication. Communication clearly identifies your beginning, process and goal. The Strategy Platform develops the successive approaches to your communication.

To develop any strategy you need to understand where you want to be at the end. Investigate as if you were writing a newspaper article about it. Asking Who? Why? What? When? Where? and How? creates the framework for identifying your strategy. On each answer, ask the same questions again. Repeat the process until all your questions are answered.

To get results, you need help. You need someone to accept your expert product on the terms offered. You will need to transfer your energy about it to another person. You will have to make the sale.

Exercise: 5Ws

- Write down what you want as a successful result for your product. It could be money, fame or being popular.
- For each item use one page of paper and answer the questions "Who? Why? What? When? Where? and How?" to achieve success with the product. Leave enough room between answers to be able to drill down with the questions again on each answer. Be specific in your answers. Greater detail will be useful in identifying the processes you will need to perform.
- Summarize the characteristics of each one on another sheet. This is the result you expect.

It is almost impossible to sell something to someone when they don't know about it. As you know by our examples, understanding the elements of something is not an easy process.

To achieve your success, you will have to raise your customer's understanding of your product. They must understand that it solves a problem or satisfies a need they have. People buy things for a reason. There are obstacles to overcome in getting to the decision to purchase something. Sometimes your customer does not know they have the problem until you offer the solution and benefits.

Money is one obstacle. One test is affordability. Can your customer afford your product? The answer to that question will depend on the financial state of the customer. The price of your product will help identify the customer for you. If you are selling an item for ten dollars, the number of potential customers, *or customer base,* will be larger than one selling for one thousand dollars. Identifying a customer's ability to pay determines your audience. Once you know your audience, you can make plans for how you will communicate to them.

Rule of Seven

The Rule of Seven is an old marketing adage. It basically says that a prospect needs to see or hear a marketing message at least seven times before buying a product. Sending a message seven times is an expectation. It could be less, or it could be more. If you need to educate your customer, then many different messages will have the Rule of Seven applied to them to achieve your success. This is a lot of messages you need your customer to hear.

Marketing extends your message or messages to your potential customers. It must be well planned to be effective. Creating a marketing plan gives you a roadmap to follow and the sales you make will determine its effectiveness.

The inputs to your marketing will be the unique advantages of the product. The message is your solution to that need. The other inputs to this platform are as many ways and types of communicating that message. The final input is the descriptive analysis of your customer or audience.

The output of this process will be a plan or series of plans that define how you convincingly communicate your message successfully resulting in a sale.

If you haven't noticed, each platform in this book, so far, acts as an input into other platforms. The better you have successfully completed the previous steps, the better your outcome. The expression "garbage in, garbage out" applies to this concept. A detailed and specific plan will achieve your expected outcome.

Exercise: Product Features and Objections

In your notebook:

- Write down a list of the unique features of your product.
- Write down a description of your customer's potential objections and a solution to them.
- Draw a line from each product feature to the objection it overcomes.
- Are there any objections without a line to a feature set? Can a feature be added to your product to address the unanswered objections? Write each down in your notebook.

Elevator Speech

The very first marketing tool you must create is a sales-oriented elevator speech. Earlier, I mentioned the elevator speech as it related to what your expert platform is. Your Strategy Platform expands the elevator speech into your sales approach.

It will need to summarize your product features and benefits and your expected result. It should summarize the unique aspects of your product and excite others about it at the same time. It needs to be concise enough to say in ten seconds. Because it is short, it should spur more conversation.

The elevator speech should get people interested. As they are more interested, they ask more questions. Most of these questions are either direct objections or related to their sales objections. It should lead you to the point of asking for a sale. Your elevator speech must be enthusiastic. You must have the energy and belief in your product that naturally becomes infectious. That viral transmission of energy starts with your elevator speech.

Does your elevator speech inspire people to ask you questions about your unique product? If it does, your elevator speech is doing its job.

Your elevator speech and drill-down answers should be living things. Update them as often as you have changes in your product. New features need to be integrated into your speech. Keeping your information fresh also keeps your enthusiasm fresh.

Marketing Plan

Traditionally there is a distinction between marketing and public relations. Public relations is a type of marketing campaign using nonpaid methods of presenting your message or brand name. Marketing usually involves some form of paid system to present your message. For our purposes here, marketing may mean either of these.

The internet presents another marketing avenue. Internet marketing campaigns take advantage of social networking tactics and/or purchased internet advertising.

A marketing campaign contains all the ways of placing your message in front of potential customers. Create a financial budget that includes the cost of all your marketing activities for the year. Once you have a marketing budget, write down all the messages you wish to get to your potential customers. Where do your customers go in real life and on line? What media do they watch? Can you send them emails?

A marketing campaign should have a stated objective. Then, the campaign should list the message type and where it will be broadcast. The frequency of the message broadcast and cost of the broadcast should be listed. Remember to regularly subtract

Exercise: Promotion

In your notebook:

- Write down a list of places you can promote your product.
- List website names that you would like to have to promote your product. Check online to see if they are available.
- Of the available sites, what typical misspellings of the site address exist? Are they available for you to own?
- Make a list of these names and buy them

the money you actually use from your budget. This will keep your remaining budget updated.

Any strategy may contain multiple strategies within the marketing plan with unique goals that combine to sell your product. Be sure to include forms of self promotion, like a website, in your plan.

Campaigns

Campaigns are subsections of your marketing plan. Usually a campaign may be used for one specific purpose, like selling one specific product. A campaign can be split into multiple messages. This provides exposure to multiple elements of a general message. Splitting a campaign can test whether one presentation works better than another in getting sales.

List each activity in your plan and the details of each activity to get the campaign completed. Identify dates and times for each activity to be started and completed. Where possible, assign a person by name or by role to the task. Provide reviews of tasks in your marketing plan and detail the results. Consistent reviews can be your best friend in keeping your activities on track. Make sure that reviews are set with enough time for there to be activities to review. A review can be used as a tool for evaluating if your current activity is meeting the goals and expectations you set for the tasks. It also allows for minor course corrections as you go.

Be careful not to over-manage what you do. Plan your expectations before starting a campaign. If you find from your reviews that you are behind schedule, or ahead of schedule, you can reset the plan and expectations.

Risk and Issues Analyses

A positive attitude comes from having your expectations met. One way to avoid having a negative ripple effect on your attitude if things go wrong is to practice risk avoidance. You must regularly look at the risks and issues that can occur. Before you even start activities, make a list of all the possible risks you could encounter. What would cause that risk to occur? This is called a trigger. If the risk did occur, what could be done to lessen the impact of the risk to your outcome?

For every possible risk, you need to write down the events that would occur to make the risk become an issue you need to fix. Also, you will need to determine the ranking of the risk. The ranking will give you a quick way to identify the likelihood of the risk to occur and the severity of the risk as an issue if it occurs. Typically, a quick red, yellow, and green identification will give a quick way to know the likelihood of the risk occurring and the severity if it became an issue. In the chart below, any risk that is green and has little chance of occurring and would have little or no impact if it did occur. Any risk with a rating that is yellow is a risk with medium impact and/or probability of occurring. A red risk is critical. A yellow or red risk will require monitoring. A red or yellow risk must be resolved as soon as possible.

A risk and issue log should be maintained regularly. Every time an issue arises, it should be logged in your risks and issues log.

Rate each issue on the risk matrix giving it a certain rating at the top and then determining its color by the severity of the risk. Once a week, look at the log of risks and issues. Are there any new risks you can add to the log? If so, what is the trigger that would cause it? How would you resolve the issue?

RISK MATRIX

		Very Low	Low	Medium	High	Very High
Likelihood of Risk Occurring	Certain	Green	Yellow	Red	Red	Red
	Very Likely	Green	Yellow	Yellow	Red	Red
	Likely	Green	Yellow	Yellow	Yellow	Red
	Not Likely	Green	Green	Green	Yellow	Yellow
	Improbable	Green	Green	Green	Green	Yellow
		Very Low	Low	Medium	High	Very High
		SEVERITY				

A method for determining the impact of a risk is as follows:

High = Very likely, the probability is more than 80%
Medium = May have an impact, the probability of it occurring is 20% to 80%
Low = Not likely to have an impact with a probability of occurrence less than 20%

Severity can be determined by the impact on your schedule. A delay to the schedule and costs should be considered part of your impact analysis.

High = A schedule delay of over 2 weeks and/or over budget by more than 10%
Medium = A schedule delay between 1 and 2 weeks and/or 5 to 10% over budget
Low = A schedule delay of less than 1 week and/or less than 5% over budget

Your action plan for potential risks is one tool that can keep your attitude positive. Identify what could go wrong and have an action plan. Develop it before the issue occurs. This keeps you from scrambling to solve a problem in a time of higher stress and anxiety.

Communication Plan

How will you communicate to your customers and potential customers? How will you communicate to yourself and your team on your plan and activities? Will you have a newsletter? Will you have a blog? How will you let your updated information reach your customer base?

Exercise: Communications

In your notebook:

- Write down a list of ways you can communicate to your customers.
- List ten blogs you can participate in where there are likely customers.

Communication is not just marketing or sales. It is simply you speaking to your audience. You want to interact with your audience regularly. Your communication should have substance. In this age of tweets and likes, it seems that every trivial event in one's life can be broadcast. Respect your audience by having something of value to share with them.

Ask your audience to help you. Sampling your potential audience will give you insights that you might not otherwise get. Do not ask too much from your audience or they may not answer any questions. Keep everything in your communications simple and short. Treat your audience as you would like to be treated.

Your written preparation before starting any tasks towards your goal will give you greater chances for success. When something goes wrong, you should have already identified it as a risk well in advance. You will know how to handle issues. The severity of an issue will also help to prioritize which issues to fix first.

Planning is your best tool to reaching your goals. Plan early and often. It is the unexpected that usually causes failure. Build a good roadmap and follow it. Your surprises will be few. You will be able to handle them with ease and little stress.

Chapter 6

THE SELLING PLATFORM

D o you remember the last thing you bought? Why did you buy it? Making a sale is a value-based proposition. The purchaser is expecting that this purchase will solve a problem or add value to their current condition.

People buy things all the time. Very often, what we buy has been influenced by a variety of factors. Price is an obvious component we look at when we buy something. Yet, there are times when the product satisfies a need that rises above the cost.

Sales Strategies

People tend to buy items from people they know and trust. Develop that trust by not always asking your audience to buy from you. In fact, I have great respect for the person who makes the communication a two-way proposition.

Develop a relationship with your potential customer that is mutual. Get to know your audience. Who is reading what you write? Why are they interested in what you have to offer? Have you made your relationship with your potential customers a personal one? Share your information in a personal way. Sharing your experiences on any subject helps your potential customer to see you as a human being with common goals and values. If they can identify with you at a personal level, you become a known commodity.

Some people will only buy their clothes at certain stores. They buy their food at certain stores. There becomes a culture of trust. Where there is trust there is a higher frequency of transactions. Sometimes people follow trusted recommendations. Word of mouth is a great way to have people find out about you. It means that someone they trust has recommended your product because of the trust you created in them. The trust gets passed from friend to friend.

As more and more people purchase goods and services online, it becomes more important to be personal. An anonymous seller is less trusted than someone with a proven track record.

On occasion, it may be an outside interest you have that attracts a person's interest first. This interest is not related to your product.

In 2009, I released a book where I had taken the entire collection of Abraham Lincoln photos and turned them into color images. The photos are in the Abraham Lincoln Presidential Library collection. They have been used for the Lincoln Bicentennial and in other Lincoln displays. The photos have been sold in the Lincoln Presidential museum and at the Gettysburg historic site.

Exercise: Other Activities

In your notebook:

- List other activities you have participated in.
- List up to three things about those activities that would interest others.

As I proceed to share this with people, they start to ask questions about the project and my interests. I can tell by their reactions that they have connected with the project's success. Almost always they ask what I am doing next. This provides me with an easy transition to discuss Success Platforms.

Closing

One of the hardest tasks for many people is asking for the sale. You will help yourself by strategizing the sales close. How will you ask for the sale? When will you ask for the sale? Identify the objections that would be raised by your customer. How can you overcome those objections in an educational and non-threatening manner before asking for the sale?

Ask for the sale more than once. If a customer says no, find out why. You may not have qualified the customer well enough to know if they need your product. You may need to educate them on how your product satisfies their needs or solves their problems.

A downsell of a similar product with some limitations may address the customer's price concerns. A product that addresses a change in marketplace or new requirements may require reeducating your customer. They may not be aware of a change in their environment.

If you have addressed your selling areas well, you need to focus on other customers. Not every customer is going to be a buyer this time.

Every time you reach out to your potential customer you are inviting them to sample your product. If more people receive the invitation, more people will likely buy your product. Include previous non-buying customers with every offer. Because they did not buy your product once, they may purchase what you offer now.

Closure Rate

Figure out your closure rate for each product. The closure rate is the number of customers who purchase divided by the number of customers approached. If you reach one thousand customers and one hundred buy, your closure rate is 10 percent. Use this number in reverse to determine how many people you have to

Exercise: Product Analysis

In your notebook:

- List all the reasons you do not buy a product.
- For each one, list anything that would have changed your mind and made you buy.
- For each of your products, use the list in number 2 to make a list of items you could include in your sales presentation to overcome objections before you reach them.

approach to reach your sales goals. If you don't have a closure rate use 10 percent as a starting point.

How much revenue do you want to receive? This is your target for your sales projections. How will it come in over each month? Is there a season when your product is in higher demand? Most brick and mortar stores have the majority of their sales in the last quarter of the year. This is because of the winter holidays. Sales of snow skiing equipment increase in winter. Sports, like golf, see increases in related sales as the weather warms up.

Conversion

Conversion is the term that describes the number of people that buy your product in relation to the number of people that received an invitation to sample it.

The number of people who buy is smaller than the number of people approached. You need to consider a few factors in determining your sales strategy.

It is time to plan for the amount of sales activity you will need to reach your goals. Take the revenue you expect to receive and divide the amount by the selling price of your product. This will give you the number of units you need to sell to reach the expected revenue. You should be able to break down the number of sales by month based on the known buying habits of your customers.

Sales Reporting

If you were to seek potential investors for your business, they would want to see a five year history of sales and projections. It only makes sense that you would have done the same exercise for yourself.

Exercise: Sales Planning

In your notebook:

- How many units do you need to sell each month to reach your sales goals?
- List the amount of hours and money you need to make these units. How many hours per month will you work on your business? How many units do you have on-hand?
- Determine if you are making a profit on selling your products. Make sure you include the cost in time and money for shipping your product. Do you have time left to make sales and market your product? If you are left with little time or money to market and sell your product, you need to revisit your Sales Platform.

Determine the profit and loss you will experience. Take the revenue you expect to receive and subtract the cost of making your product as well as the cost of doing business. This is your profit or loss you can expect from doing business.

Some businesses expect a loss for a certain amount of time. Remember the Amazon example? The business operated at a loss with the intention of creating a position as the first source customers would use to purchase books.

Diversification

Diversification of products or services can be one strategy to reach a significant revenue figure. If you are building a business with the potential for multiple products, it is helpful to build a product line. Using the Sales Platform and your expected closure rate, build your product catalog in line with meeting your expected sales goals.

If your sales strategy includes more than one product be sure to provide added value to your products. There should be a progression of value and increased benefit as you move through your Sales Platform. Always have a product you can add to say thank you to your customers.

Design your sales strategy to upsell to your customer. Your Sales Platform of products must have a natural progression of added information or added value. Using a Sales Platform you can increase your sales to a customer who is already buying from you.

A customer who has purchased from you is one who has overcome their own purchasing objections. They have a relationship of trust with you. Always have something else they will need to buy.

When I was a young boy in the Midwest, there was a salesman from a woolen mill in Minnesota who traveled house to house selling winter coats, blankets and sweaters. Every year my mother bought a number of items for each member of the family. Similar products were available in local stores, but we looked forward to the yearly visit by this salesman. Every year there was some new product that was brought out at the end of the sale. It was always a limited run of something. Every year it was added to the sale. There was a personal relationship with the salesman.

Build the personal relationship with your customer. This includes after the sale. Every customer issue, complaint, or return is an opportunity for you. Your expertise is one of the things that made them purchase from you. Share your expert knowledge.

Rebuilding your relationship with an unhappy customer is also important. A satisfied customer will come back and purchase from you again, if treated well. A customer with a problem that is solved agreeably has been transformed into a satisfied customer. Develop your customer service policy as part of your sales strategy. A customer treated well in customer service will buy your products again.

Things always change. Update your sales approach based on new information or new trends. With the social media world, new information can very often go viral. Can you develop new products that tie in to viral events?

Quirky presentations often are enough to make you and your product stick in your customer's heads. People tend to share cute things. When I was a music director, there was one promotion representative for a major record company who used the term "my man" with everyone. If something exceptional occurred with his current product, you moved to being his "main man of all main men". This was just quirky enough to be remembered. Indeed, I have jokingly used the phrase myself since then.

Review and Update

Review your sales catalogue and sales approach at least quarterly. Ask your customers to tell you what they think quarterly. Keep an email list of customers and potential customers. Stay in touch with them. Share information with them. Keep them, informed. Ask them what they need.

Update your sales projections every month. Update any changes to the cost of doing business. Update projections to reflect a potential increase or drop in sales. Indicate why you expect this change to occur. Everything runs in cycles and has ups and downs. Your success will depend on your regular planning.

Chapter 7

YOUR PUBLICITY PLATFORM

O ne most obvious platform to conquer is getting known or publicity. Your Communication Platform touched on publicity. This is a subject with enough complexity that it is indeed a platform itself.

The power of the press and media is amazing. In the past few years, reality television shows have taken reasonably average people and, by their appearance on the shows, made them media celebrities. Celebrity, fame, and notoriety all put people in the spotlight. Once in that spotlight, marketing becomes easier. It also comes with increased costs to maintain it and a loss of privacy.

Publicity requires activity. Executing properly focused activities will expose your message to other people. Publicity campaigns are used to organize multiple activities to promote specific products, names or goals. In a campaign, a series of activities focused on a particular message are executed. As with all platforms, planning and documentation are the tools that keep you on track.

Publicity often requires a budget for determining the amount and types of publicity that can be performed. While there are some activities that have little or no cost, your success will depend on reaching the largest audience of potential customers. This will mean you must spend money.

Publicity is a broad subject. There are entire books written on the subject. Entire businesses are devoted to publicity. Public relations and advertising firms look at all of the available channels for delivering a message. They provide a mix of messages and channels aimed at presenting the message to the largest number of people for the available budget.

Publicity and the Internet

With the rise of the Internet, the number of avenues for promoting yourself and your goals has increased. In fact, Internet publicity has become its own discipline.

You may find yourself in the position of needing to acquire some level of marketing expertise. In the end, you will be responsible for the message, media channels and delivery of your publicity campaigns. While others may do the work, you will sign off on everything.

I have been in broadcasting and advertising in my previous careers. Having an understanding of media creation, copywriting and marketing statistics has been invaluable in making choices and knowing when to pull a campaign that is not providing results.

Publicity can use advertising, public relations and Internet Marketing to achieve the desired goals. In public relations you will use press releases, magazine or newspaper articles, blogs and any other free vehicle to transmit your message. The key to successful public relations is the ability for your message to be rebroadcast. Your public relations information becomes the published product for newspapers, magazines, radio and television. These media outlets have the same goal that you do, that is, to get more eyes on their content. This requires that your information be timely and interesting. Getting attention is the key.

In the late 1960s, Jay Ward, the creator of the Rocky and Bullwinkle series, had developed a publicity stunt to get media attention. Ward had purchased an island in Minnesota and had named it Moosylvania. Ward and his team of writers drove their Moosylvania bus cross country, gathering signatures on a petition for Moosylvania statehood. They planned to arrive at the White House and deliver the petition to then President Kennedy. Unknown to Ward and crew, the Cuban Missile crisis was unfolding at that moment. The Moosylvania contingent was removed from the White House grounds under gunpoint.

Publicity requires that you get the attention of your audience. Sometimes it requires getting their attention more than once. Remember the Rule of Seven says a person remembers something after seven exposures. Your message falls under this rule. Nothing in the Rule of Seven says it has to be the exact wording each time. Varying the delivery a little bit each time helps to capture the attention of your target audience.

Negative Publicity

People like to share bits of information that they find interesting. Sometimes negative publicity gets the attention. Sometimes the odd and quirky or unusual activity gets attention.

A lawsuit or an arrest of a celebrity brings them into the media spotlight. Sometimes negative publicity regenerates interest in a celebrity and can even revive a career. The comedian Joan Rivers chained herself to a shopping cart at warehouse store in Los Angeles. Bullhorn in hand, she urged customers to make the store carry her book. She was arrested at the request of the store management and escorted away. The story was national news for a day.

Negative publicity can be just a first shot in a series of planned activities. The goal is to reshape public opinion. A series of events can show how a person or cause has changed. Popular opinion about that person or subject is favorably changed.

Public Relations

Public relations is a non-commercial activity. You don't purchase the vehicle to deliver your message. Instead, you provide information directly to broadcast media to be integrated into news or entertainment programs.

Press releases take a specific event, alliance or item of noteworthiness and deliver it to media organizations. You want to create the impression of getting the notice because of some valid reference from a third party. Getting a quote from a famous person or an authority on the subject into your press release adds to your authenticity.

Radio and television interviews give you the opportunity to be seen and/or heard telling your story. Remember that media outlets need to fill the airwaves with something that will attract an audience. They make their money by showing advertisers how many people actually tune in to their programming. You should be able to make a compelling argument in your media packet or press release for putting you on the air. If your presentation is not interesting, your message is not interesting.

Forming an alliance with a charitable organization adds both credibility and newsworthiness. In the United States, broadcast organizations are required to show documented evidence of their community involvement as a part of their broadcast license renewal process. Contact the community affairs director of your local stations. He or she should be aware of your charitable event or activity. Reference your involvement briefly and, then, refocus on the charitable event.

One reason for calling media outlets is to create a relationship with the key people. Get to know the people whom you send information. Ask for their guidance to get your message used by them. Have a charitable tie-in they can use. Show how your message tied in with a charity helps to fulfill the community involvement requirements they must meet as broadcasters.

If your message is a newsworthy item, create a video showing you and/or someone representing the charity answering questions. Send the video and the written questions to the news room. Especially in smaller media markets, this technique allows their reporter to appear to be interviewing you.

When the Beatles were at their most popular, radio stations would get an audio tape of each Beatle answering a question. The local announcer would record the questions. The result was an impression that the Beatles were in the studio.

Focus on all media types. Radio provides opportunities for plugging your product in interview situations. Television often

Exercise: Product Uniqueness

In your notebook:

- Write down a list of interview questions you might be asked about your product. Remember to use the 5Ws to develop your questions.

- Write down what makes your product unique? What makes it timely? Identify what makes your message the best message for the media to broadcast.

- Make a list of the broadcaster's goals in broadcasting your message. This will give you the arguments to overcome any objections.

- List ways you can make your message unique. Is there a way to make your audio or video presentation a candidate for viral exposure?

- List all the newspapers in your area and write a press release for each one.

---

focuses on entertainment values that minimize your product message. Creatively bring the attention back to your product while delivering the entertainment values.

Newspapers are still alive. Find out the editorial needs of your papers and fill them. Find a local angle to your story to make it more appealing to editors. Reach out to small and large papers. They all need content.

Internet Video

Video sharing on the Internet gives another way to publish video about your message. Remember that once you post your video, it will likely stay there forever. Post video content online with caution. You must be sure that your presentation is flawless. If you have any doubt about the perfection of your video, do not share it. Rework your video presentations until they are perfect.

In general, only publish the **best** representation of you and your message. Your audience needs to be completely won over by all aspects of your message. Give your audience every reason to love you. You are making an impression on your audience. If you wanted to impress a potential employer in an interview, you would present yourself in the best possible light. Think of media presentations as a job interviews. Always do your best.

Your message is the input to the Publicity Platform. There are planning, creative and placement activities. You will also have a budget to create and maintain. The output will be your messages appearing online and in the media.

The Ratings Game

Radio and television stations survive on ratings and sales. In radio, Arbitron ratings determine relative rankings of radio stations. Estimates of listenership for specific age ranges and time periods come from listenership surveys. Television has Neilsen ratings that deliver similar information.

The geographic reach of a broadcast signal also needs to be considered. Purchasing advertising requires that you reach the largest number of people for each dollar spent. Be creative in setting up the placement of advertising. Is it more effective to advertise on five lower ranked stations than the number one station in a market? Find out if there are stations located in a suburb or neighboring market. If they reach into your advertising market, add them to your mix.

Finally, match your message to the station's format. Make sure the average viewer or listener to a station would likely be interested in your product. If you are buying advertising, often a sales executive will help you build your advertising information. You can use this to develop your mix of stations. Use more than one advertisement with the same message to send your message in different ways.

Sometimes purchasing advertising can be an advantage in getting non-advertising placement. A station may consider an interview on the news program if you are also airing commercials. Make sure you can be interviewed in a newsworthy manner. An interview should not be directly matched to the advertising. Your interviews must be entertaining and relevant.

There are formats where the interview is the entertainment. Talk radio or television is always looking to book the best and most interesting guest. They want someone who will get the audience to respond. Every show has its producer or producers. These people screen potential guests and act as the go-between for the host and guest. The producer is your best friend or worst enemy. You need to be able to pitch the producer on your message. Use your best elevator speech in presenting yourself to a producer. Producers are always on the lookout for a good guest. Keep the audio or video of your interviews. Use them in your press kit. Put them on your website or public websites if they are good. Only use the best online.

Internet Presence

Because media posted online has an eternal lifespan, be consistent. Make sure the message you send out today will be consistent with a message you send out in five or ten years. Your potential audience will find the inconsistencies in your message.

Develop a web presence as a part of your publicity platform. You will need to have a web page that promotes you. Your name should be the address your customer types into the browser. The address with a ".com" at the end is the best. You should also have a webpage for your product. Host a blog on your page. Write a consistent message as often as you can. This helps in keeping your page relevant. Internet promotion is geared towards search engine results. Everyone wants to be on the first page of the search engine results. SEO or Search Engine Optimization is critical for your online publicity. Learn as much as you can about SEO and Internet Marketing.

Marketing Plan

The output of your Publicity Platform activities is a marketing plan. Start your marketing plan by listing the results you desire. Define the message, audience and media you will use. For each media type, list the message and when it will be broadcast. Identify the audience's age, gender and income. Identify your expected return on investment. Set a goal for the amount of money that you expect to make in sales for each dollar spent in advertising.

Track your budget and what each ad costs. Make sure you do not go over your budget. If you are out of advertising money, try public relations.

For public relations campaigns, track what you send, to whom and how you send it. Identify what you are doing to stand out of the crowd. List the community or charity tie-in. Identify the television, radio and newspaper outlets you will contact. Create a schedule for each press release or news story you send out.

Log each expected Internet submission and the type of submission it is. Create a list of notifications you will send to other websites indicating you've put something on the web.

List the blog postings you expect to write to support the campaign.

When you are done, you should have a written plan for every type of publicity submission in your campaign. It should be scheduled and have contacts listed where you might follow up with someone. Schedule as much as you can in your planning. The plan should be able to be followed. Modify your plan as necessary. If something new fits your message and is easy to insert into your plan, make the adjustment.

Publicity is an ongoing activity. Make your plan and stick to it. Review it regularly and if any element is not working, stop using it. As early as possible evaluate your paid advertising for success. If it is not working cut your losses and stop that advertising.

Never stop promoting. The more people that get your message, the more success you have.

Chapter 8

YOUR MENTORING PLATFORM

A chieving success is rarely a solo function. When I was still in college, I made the decision to work in radio. I was working as an intern and became friends with one of the announcers. He later became my mentor and brought me in to his new radio station as a Music Director.

The mentoring relationship is a unique relationship. A mentor has skin in the game. There is a commitment to the success of the person being mentored. Mentors provide counseling and guidance. A mentor will share a lifetime of experience. The mentor will guide you based on a unique relationship between you. Achieving success becomes a source of pride for all involved.

Coaching

Coaching is a different relationship. The differences between mentoring and coaching are frequently misunderstood.

Sometimes a mentor will not charge for his or her time. Some mentors have made mentoring a part of their Product Platform. Mentors provide ongoing guidance that is aimed at achieving many consecutive goals. There is often a mutual friendship between the two. Rarely does a person have more than one mentor at once.

Coaches, on the other hand, are there to achieve a specific result. The goal may be to teach a specific technique or to develop a specific document or plan. Compensation is usually required for achieving each goal. A coach may or may not continue through multiple goals.

Some types of coaching are long term arrangements. A life coach may spend months working with a client. There is the expectation that the coach will no longer be required after reaching a goal.

Coaching is a good thing. No one knows everything. A coach can provide training and guidance to master specific techniques. I think of coaching as a necessary business expense. A coach can help you be productive. When there is new information to learn, you can spend many hours learning new tasks. A coach can streamline the time spent on a task. Ideally, learn how to do the task as a result of working with a coach. If your budget does not allow it, add more time to your planning for new activities. At best, triple your expected work in your plan.

Training

Training is a type of coaching. It lacks the one-on-one character of traditional coaching. The focus is teaching specific tasks to achieve a single goal. Often many people are trained at once on the same topic. It is often a less costly way to get knowledge and capabilities. Because the attention of the teacher is divided between many students, unique advice specific to one individual may not be available.

When I researched my first book, a history of Abraham Lincoln, I discovered that early one room school sessions used reciting out loud to learn addition and English. Each student was reading a different course of study. This led to a distracting atmosphere of noise that made learning harder. Make sure that you focus during trainings. The rule of seven applies to you too. Keep distractions to a minimum.

Instructor led learning to a class of many people is less likely to have the same result as individual training. Multiple people add to the level of distraction in a course.

The opportunity to receive guidance from someone with more experience in any discipline is valuable. Be willing to shop for the best value in your coaching and instruction.

Because I am a certified project manager, I am required to take a specified number of hours of associated professional activity every three years. I research all the available training. Based on all the available options, I find that the cost varies widely for the same information.

Instruction is possible to find at varying costs. Research and check references before you purchase any instruction.

Coaching is a bit different. A coach's professional reputation may be enough to select a coach. It is still worth the effort to research and check references. There are often opportunities to see a coach present some introductory information at a live event or online.

A teleseminar is an instructional course. They are streamed on line to many students at once and often are recorded. The disadvantage to a recorded seminar is that you cannot get clarifications or ask questions. Live teleseminars have text based chat to communicate with the instructor. Questions are answered in the live video stream by the instructor.

Peer Mentoring

You should have a peer mentoring group. Some call this a mastermind group. Your peer mentoring group should be a collection of people who have similar goals and activities. Since a multitude of opinions can lead to new ideas, this group will be your brainstorming team. They will also act as a support network for question and sometimes moral support.

Brainstorming is the free exchange of ideas that are proposed without any judgment to their applicability or value to your current problem. There are various ways to record brainstorming information. There is a mastermind recording technique. A simple list of the ideas can give you a starting point for your discussions.

Each item in your list then starts to be examined. Identify any flaws to resolving a problem using each item. Those that provide potential solutions get further analysis. Identify all the tasks that will execute the idea. Look at the risks and issues for each one. Choose the ideas with the greatest likelihood of success.

Your peer mentoring group can also help you identify your target audiences. You can use their input to give you options on any item that you have difficulty resolving.

Make sure that your peer mentoring group does not get too large. You can have multiple peer mentoring groups. You may also find that you need to add or remove people from your peer mentoring. Keep your peer mentoring group as an open and fluid organization. Find those people that work together well. You want ideas and sound judgment from the members.

Exercise: Mentoring Prospects

In your notebook:

- Write down a list of people you might invite to join your peer mentoring group.
- Write down names of people who might be mentors to you.

Your mentoring platform should provide you with the support at varying levels to be able to learn new information, receive support and new ideas when you are faced with unknowns or issues. If you are lucky enough to have a mentor, in the true sense of the term, then you will have an individual in your corner for the long term.

Chapter 9

THE ACTIVITY PLATFORM

You have to act on all the plans you put together. Plans should be the skeleton for your activities. They are a blueprint for what and when you will accomplish tasks to achieve your goal.

There are phases that define the types of activities. Everything you do towards achieving a goal is a project. To remember the classic phases of a project, I use the phrase "Ideas properly executed can continue". The first letter of each work is the first letter of each phase.

The phases of a project are inception, planning, execution, control, and closing. The transition from one phase to another will offer a natural point to pause and evaluate your goal, what has been done and what is left to achieve the goal.

IDEAS	→	INCEPTION
PROPERLY	→	PLANNING
EXECUTED	→	EXECUTION
CAN	→	CONTROL
CONTINUE	→	CLOSING

You should be able to define the completed tasks and specific documents that are expected at the end of each phase. At the end of each phase, stop. Evaluate the phase. If there are no problems, continue to the next phase.

Phase Gates

The process of stopping at the end of each phase is called a phase gate. Each phase gate provides an opportunity to stop and revise or refine your plans. Use each phase as a reference point to check your progress. Make sure you have done all the work to reach your goal. If not, you may need to revise your plan. You may not be ready to move forward. You may need to do some extra work to reach your goal.

Reevaluate your risks and issues as part of the transition between phases. Verify that your initial assumptions about achieving your goal have not changed.

Every phase will have one or more inputs. Each phase will have one or more processes performed with one or more outputs. Outputs may be a document or a preparation for another phase. Make sure you have the outputs you expect at the end of each phase.

The end of each phase is a natural point to pause. In business, each phase ends with a go or no-go decision. There is no disgrace in choosing a no-go on your projects. It may simply mean that getting to your current goal will take more time and work. If there are serious risks or issues, this is the time to rethink your strategy. Plans can be changed if there is a valid reason.

Project Planning

Project planning is important. Break your plan into one section for each of the five phases. A project plan is not just the list of tasks you intend to perform. It is all the plans you have made for reaching your goal combined. Each phase has clear inputs, process and outputs.

Inception

Inception covers the activities related to conceiving your goal. Your mind platform is an input to the inception phase. Your goals are also an input to inception. You should be able to document your expected result. Your charter should answer three questions. Why am I doing this? Who will participate in the activities? What defines success?

Define the scope of your work. Make it a clearly defined result. When you plan your activities, limit them to only actions that provide the scope you defined. Hold the defined scope without change. Do not allow your scope to change while you are working to a goal.

Exercise: Charter Review

In your notebook:

- Review the charter you wrote in the Mind Platform chapter.
- Update your charter as needed with any new information.

Your elevator speech should be the next thing you complete. Think of the elevator speech as a radio commercial. It is possible to combine your elevator speech and charter. Your elevator speech must be interesting. It should make the listener stop and ask questions about what you are saying.

Tell your listener who you are and your background. Clearly state your vision or goals. Share your reasons for wanting these goals.

Elevator speeches need to stand out. Is there a way to make your elevator speech different? Maybe ask an unusual question tied to your subject. If your elevator speech is going to be shared by video, you might want to use bright colors to get attention. In most cases, you will be giving your elevator speech without any notice or planning. You need to be able to get the listener's attention on your own.

Know who your audience will be. Tailor your speech to that audience. When you test your speech find someone who would be a likely customer. Identify the interesting parts of your speech. Find out what you can improve. Clearly targeting your speech will help you succeed.

Your charter should have your goal and product clearly defined. Review it and see if you can make a list of each part. Make sure you identify the benefits of what you are offering in your speech. What problem does it solve?

Identify the strengths of each element of your speech. Share who you are and how you got here. Tell some of your back story with enough time left to make your pitch.

What makes your audience interested in your speech? Why are you telling your story to her or him?

What ideas can you brainstorm about yourself or your goal? Decide which of those ideas are memorable. Which ideas stick with people? Use only the ideas that stand out. Build your elevator speech around these ideas.

Brainstorm your elevator speech ideas with other people in your field and people who know you. Make changes to your elevator speech using the strongest elements. Have a thirty second speech that can stand alone. Keep your speech under one hundred words. Also, prepare a sixty second and a ninety second elevator speech. Each thirty second segment should be under one hundred words. I like to have the longer speeches that add depth to the original thirty second speech. An elevator speech must have a single message.

Post your charter and elevator speech where you will see them often. There is an old saying that it is hard to remember that your goal was to drain the swamp when you are up to your knees in alligators. The constant reminders of goals help us stay on track. Place more than one copy on your walls.

Exercise: Elevator Speech

In your notebook:

- Brainstorm all the ideas you can about your goals and yourself.
- Write your thirty second elevator speech. Continue to refine your speech until you have a compelling speech that tells who you are and where you are going. Show why you are unique. Identify what your offer is to your listener. What do you want the listener to do as a result of your speech?

Planning

The planning phase defines the activities and events that you must act on to get to your goal. Do you have enough resources to complete your plan? How much money is in your budget? How much time do you have to reach your goals? If you have a product involved, is there a seasonal sales period you must reach?

Will you have any legal requirements to start? Have you incorporated or created some legal entity to protect yourself? If not, add this to your tasks.

Make a list of all the tasks you will need to perform to reach your goal. If you are able to put them into a computer, you can rearrange the list so that they are in order. It also allows tasks to be added or removed easily. Mobile Apps and cloud computing will let you build plans on your phone or tablet.

Each task should have a start and end date. Find the duration of each task by counting the number of days from start to finish. Write the duration next to each task. Identify any tasks that can occur at the same time. List each task by its priority. Take all the tasks that depend on each other. Add the duration of each task and you will have the duration for each phase. All the phases added together tell you how long it should be to reach your goal.

My preference is to have each item in a column. If one item requires a series of tasks to complete it, list them below it. Indent each to show it is related to the main item. If you have other people doing the work for a task, you can add their names in another column. This helps to identify any task relying on another person. It also helps to plan when you will check on the readiness or progress of any task.

Go over each item and identify where a risk may occur. Make a list of each risk. List why that risk may occur in the next column. In a third column, list the possible causes that would change the risk to an issue. What would be the severity of the risk? How likely is it to occur? If it did occur, what would be the effect on your plan?

Issues are risks that have occurred. What issues are you facing at the start of your activity? Write down a list of each issue. Will it cause a high impact to your plan? Will it have a medium or low impact? List ways you can fix the issue or make the issue not have an impact on your plan.

This is your risk and issue log. You should review this at least every week. If something new becomes a risk or issue, add it your list. This prepares you for unexpected events. If you don't plan for the unexpected, it can affect your plans and affect your outlook. A positive outlook is the result of good planning.

A communication plan identifies your reporting. A status report listing the main accomplishments and issues for each week of your activity is a valuable tool. You can use this to focus yourself weekly. If you have others involved in your plan, a status gives everyone a view into the current activities of your plan.

Budgets are critical to meeting your goals. Every item or service should be listed with the estimated cost of each. Where you can get quotes for an item or service, record the amount and provider. Look for quality results at a fair price. If there is a guarantee or warranty, record it.

A contact list should be developed with the names and contact information of everyone working on the tasks. It should be easily found by anyone on your team.

Execution

The most exciting part of your plan is executing it. It can also be the most challenging. You will be doing all the work in this phase. You will get quotes for work to be performed. Your team and subcontractors will be brought together. Tasks are assigned and acted on at the proper times.

Each completed task will need to be evaluated for completeness and overall quality. Each part of your plan should be done the very best it can. You are responsible for the quality. Everything you do must be the best.

When I was a project manager at a health insurance company, we developed software fixes using a labor team overseas. For months, we would come to a standard review at the end of every week and find that portions of the work were not done or not done to our quality standards. I suggested a shorter review cycle to help us keep schedules. Using this technique we were able to identify problems early. We fixed the problems to bring the project back on schedule. Use creative solutions to keep your project on schedule.

Follow your communication plans. Update the risks and issues regularly. Mark each completed task so you know what is left to do. When anything in your planning does not make sense, adjust it until it does.

Controlling

Controlling looks at the scope, schedule, costs, risks and issues of the project at each review point. In most cases, a weekly review will be enough to verify that you are under the limits you set to reach your goal. If something should happen that would cause you to change any aspect of your plans, use a change control process to record it. Write down the change and what it affects.

If it impacts your budget, you may need to add more money to your budget. If it requires a faster result, you may need to add more people to do the work.

This is the concept of triple constraint. A balanced plan defines the resources (people doing the work), the cost and the time to complete a project. A change to any of the three triple constraints causes an increase in the others to retain balance. If you need to change from your plan made in the planning phase, count on increasing one or all of the other elements in the triple constraint.

Closure

Closure is one of the most overlooked phases of any goal based activity. Closure helps you identify what went right or wrong in what you did. We all learn by mistakes. There is pride in our accomplishments. Make sure you document the lessons you have learned. Repeat the activities that worked well. The problem items should be on your next risk list.

Finally, pay all your bills. Complete any final administrative items. Acknowledge your team. Send thank you letters that acknowledge their efforts. Enjoy your success.

Chapter 10

THE ONLINE PLATFORM

I n the past one hundred fifty years, the world has changed a number of times. As I have mentioned, I am a devotee of Abraham Lincoln and the American Civil War. The fact that Lincoln embraced the new technology of his time was critical to the success of the Union Army in the early 1860s. New technology included the telegraph and the photograph. Lincoln spent much of his time in the Telegraph office during the war. The photographer was the techno-geek of his day. For the first time, use of balloons meant that man could fly. All of this changed the world at the time.

Technology has changed our lives forever. Today, your customers are online. Whether they use their smart phone, tablet, reader or a computer, they are online. As a result, a new field of promotional activity has emerged. It cannot be ignored. Reaching an online audience is a critical marketing technique.

Communication by the written word, audio, or video is instant. We all have email accounts and Facebook pages. We can tweet our thoughts instantly to the world to as many followers as we have signed up. We connect to the business world through LinkedIn.

Social media has changed the playing field. Radio and television are no longer the exclusive sources of media broadcasting. Video is delivered by television stations and websites. Smart phones and tablets play videos on demand. You Tube hosts millions of videos that stream with a single click of a mouse. The elite status of traditional media is lost. We are all able to be broadcasters. Our videos, emails, tweets and any other media messages compete for everyone's time and attention.

It is easy to have your message ignored online or just lost in the crowd. There is so much competition that some businesses exist solely to get a message to stand out on the Internet. Just to be able to complete, you must have a presence on the Internet. For every business, you will need one or more web addresses related to your message. Each will have one or more web pages.

Exercise: Social Media

- Review the types of web communication you currently do. List each blog or other web information you create.
- List how often you update your social media by type.
- Find the ranking of the sites you participate in.
- List any of these sites that are blacklisted. Remove them from your web strategy. Delete any old listings if you can.

Getting Found

A list of email addresses becomes your key to reaching enough people to share your message successfully. There are two methods for getting people to sign up for your list, paid or organic (free). Paid advertisements target specific markets by advertising on websites. The free method requires that you get your website to be in the top results of a search on the Internet.

The search engine is the king of Internet placement. Google is the current number one search engine. At the time of this writing, over 66% of all searches are done on Google. Over 2.5 billion searches are made by people worldwide every day.

The ability to reach this many people from a Google search will drive your ability to sell your product. The amount of results returned by any search is also awesome. Your message without any planning is just one of thousands to millions of returned results.

The critical question is how your message will be seen by the most people. When your key topic is the result of a search, it should be on the first page.

The number one result from a search gets over 36% of the clicks. Number two and three were clicked 12.5% and 9.5% of the time respectively.[3]

The total clicks on the number one result are equal to all the clicks for numbers two, three, four and five. In fact, ranking on the first page gives roughly eight times the click through response than page two. The importance of getting your message to the top of the search engine results is obvious.

---

3   **Top Google Result Gets 36.4% of Clicks [Study]** by Danny Goodwin, April 21, 2011, http://searchenginewatch.com/article/2049695/Top-Google-Result-Gets-36.4-of-Clicks-Study

Keywords

As you may have guessed, getting to the coveted first page of a Google search result is not easy. Keywords determine if your information will be included in search results.

A keyword is a word or phrase that is typed into a search engine. Each web page has keywords assigned to it. You or your web designer will place these keywords into the top code and title of the webpage. This keyword is one of the factors that a search engine will use to include a web address in a search result.

Google provides tools to help you understand the popularity of specific keywords. Google links keywords to their paid Adwords program, but finding keywords is the same process for free searches. Just entering "keyword tool" in the search box on Google will give you a direct link to the tool.

Google has many tools to help you. The Google Keyword Tool Box has the current version of all the tools available for keywords as well as other tools. Each summary in the tool box has direct links to the tool in the description. You can find keywords and what's currently trending on the Internet. Finding a search keyword that has a high volume is crucial. You will notice that search volumes are worldwide. This means that your audience is potentially anywhere in the world. Remember this when you define your target audience. Your customer is as likely to be in India as in the United States.

Google will help you learn about keywords and almost anything. Google has video tutorials and tools in Google itself. Others are on You Tube. There are also online forums where you can learn about the search engine optimization, or SEO, and many other things related to Internet Marketing.

If you want to know anything, like how to get free traffic, just type it into Google. Google's search results are often a good place to start your education.

Free ranking in search results also requires back links. To make a back link, you may blog or respond to a blog with a link to your site and/or text.

Google's stated intention is to reward social networking. Back links provide a contextual basis for Google to rate the relevance of your site. Google has a formula for determining the relevance of a website. The higher the relevance rating from Google, the higher that website ranks in the Google search results.

As an example, expert sites are ranked higher than others. Expert sites contain a minimum of twenty pages of relevant content. You must have unique information that meets the content of your key word subject matter. In fact, Google can punish you for duplicate content on your websites or blogs.

Google can and will change the rules without notice. They are in the business of making money from placing advertising on relevant websites. They want Google ads on a website that you will click. It would make sense that Google results are returned based upon the relevance that someone would click on a Google advertisement.

Paid Placement

Paid search placement allows you to choose a keyword and other parameters that set how your message will be shown. Your paid message shows up as an ad on a variety of pages. If someone clicks on your ad, you will be charged the agreed upon price for each click. This is called pay-per-click (PPC advertising).

Cost estimates and keyword traffic for PPC in its search engine results are provided by Google. This helps to plan your marketing. Payment options will vary by country and currency.

The pay-per-click model is also used on other websites with high traffic. Budgets are very important when you spend money for online advertising. It is easy to spend a lot of money and not see results. Test with small amounts of money to see if you are getting the results you want.

The Mailing List is Key

The goal of all your efforts is to have a large mailing list focused on the market you are targeting. Make sure that you stay on track. If you are an author, you want a mailing list of potential buyers of your book. If you sell flowers, you want a list of people who will buy flowers from you.

There are many videos and trainings on Internet marketing available. Some are free and some cost money. Learn everything you can about SEO (Search Engine Optimization). Understand what Internet Marketing efforts are. If you decide not to do this work yourself, you should know what it takes to get results from these activities.

While a mailing list is important, it is important that you do not have unsolicited contacts. There are laws against such things. The CAN-SPAM Act in the US and Europe controls the things you can and cannot do in acquiring names for mailings. Getting a mailing list requires that you have a specific request from everyone who signs up for your mailings. A second verification of each request to be added to your list must be made. This double opt-in guarantees that each information request be verified. Make sure you always get a double opt-

Exercise: Contacts

- Make a list of all your contacts from emails or other social media.
- What is ten percent of your total list? This is your base list sales potential.
- Multiply the potential sales list by the price of your lowest product. This is current sales potential.

in to comply with the CAN-SPAM Act or you may lose your website altogether.

Spam is sending emails to addresses without permission or a request. Sending emails found to be spam is not good. Complaints of spam contacts affect your status on the Internet. In addition, your emails are lost to your potential customer. You want to have a good relationship with your targeted audience. At worst, spam emails can cause problems with your business relationships.

Communicating with your subscribers by email is done through an autoresponder. An autoresponder service will get your customer's name and email address from the sales or sign-in page. It will send them to a webpage that asks them to verify the sign-up request in their email. Once they click the verification link, they have verified twice that they want to receive your mailings. This is your double opt-in.

You will need to create your initial opt-in sales page. Keep the sign in portion of your sales page simple. If you have directed your audience to a separate opt-in page from a sales page, you need only a place for the customer to put in their name and email address and enough text to ask for the information. This is often followed by a big arrow pointing to the entry fields.

The strategy is to get the customer to opt in. Once they completed the opt in, you have a great opportunity to maintain their interest. If you have acquired this customer from a sales page, then you have an opportunity to sell them another product. If you are using your list to sell a product later, this is an opportunity to give them something. This one time opportunity, or OTO, should have some urgency attached to it. Call your customer to action because you have a deadline for their participation. Urge them to click that button now. If you offer a sales item and your customer does not buy it, offer them a similar product with a reduced feature set at a lower price.

Allow your online customers to get to know you. Have at least three free items of interest to give to your potential customers before you ask them to buy. You might even be getting their email by offering something free. Give them an opportunity to buy something they need. Once your customer has bought something from you, offer them another product from your sales funnel. A previous customer no longer has objections to buy from you.

Keep your customers engaged. Also, keep yourself relevant as part of that process. Refresh your strategies for reaching your target audience often. Blogging, creating videos or any other communication keeps you in front of your target audience.

A year before I started writing Success Platforms, I signed up for the Internet marketing programs that were of interest to me. I have received over thirty-six thousand emails as a result. This is an example of the amount of information your target audience receives. This is why it is so important to create campaigns that reach as many people as possible with the information they will easily see as useful and important.

Use the information that search engines and autoresponders provide to determine the success of what you are doing.

Determine how many people look at your offer and actually click on the button to get your offer. This is called the click through rate. You want to have as many people click through to your opt-in page. Change your offers and web pages until you have the results you want.

Psychology of Sales

Learn all you can about the psychology of sales. If you know what makes a person purchase something, then your ability to stand out is increased. Your target audience is seeking information. They are trying to solve some urgent problem. Let them know how you can help them.

Share the successes that come from your product. Have test cases and show how they have been successful. Show the value of your product to your customer. Include a monetary value for these successes. Show what you would have paid to someone else to have this result.

Your Online Platform requires that you embrace the web. You should be a part of Twitter, Facebook, Google Plus or any other web presence website. You must participate to succeed. If you are lucky enough to have one or more of your online postings go viral, your visibility rises. Use all kinds of media. Write blogs. Create videos and send tweets. Join online organizations. Wherever possible have a page on each social network site devoted to you and your products. Let people know where you will be speaking. Put videos of your speeches online.

Rule of Thirds

Find balance in your social networking. Use the Rule of Thirds to give balance to your online presence. One third of you social media postings should focus on you and your business.

Share your professional accomplishments. Write about your business advances.

One third of your posts should be about you or your business based on information from outside sources, that is, the information you have found interesting as you focus on your business. New statistics or information in your field is a good example. Keep your information current. Rewrite what you have read to avoid any duplicate content penalties. The last third should be interactive. Answer questions and interact with other web-readers. Ask questions. Get conversations going online. Be an interactive part of websites related to your Expert Platform.

Success is a result of successfully contacting people who can benefit from you and your product. Get guidance where you need it. When time is important, use consultants or coaches to get your message online. Compare the cost of doing the work yourself or using the services of a coach. Put a money value on your time. It will make your decisions easier. There are many proven techniques for your online presence. There are always new ideas, too. Be creative. Keep learning and you will find new audiences. You may even find new products.

Chapter 11

THE PERFORMANCE PLATFORM

You must have some way to determine if you are successful. It is important to know if your activities are getting you to your goals. You must have a plan for measuring your results.

At the beginning of your planning, you can identify what you expect as a result of your efforts. Identify the planned value that you expect at the end of the project. For all the work planned, you should be able to place a dollar value on it.

Put the duration or the number of hours you expect for completing each task. Every task should have an hourly rate attached to it. Multiply the number of hours by that rate to get the planned value for the task. Add the budgeted costs of all the tasks to get the planned value for the project. You can also do this for subsets of the work performed. This helps you plan when you will use up portions of your budget.

Include a checkpoint in your activities. Most businesses use a weekly checkpoint to review the past week's work. At each weekly checkpoint, compare your planned value against what you actually spent. You will be able to identify your budget spent and future needs.

Use the time to update your list of risks and issues. Keep track of the number of issues and risks that you identify over time. If they go up, you need to look at the causes. Your risks and issues should stay the same or go down over time.

Monetary Value of Risk

You can calculate the expected monetary value of a risk occurring by multiplying the likelihood of a risk occurring by the cost of fixing the problem. If you expect there is a 25% likelihood of an error occurring and it will cost $1,000 to fix it, then the expected monetary value of the risk is $250. For all your potential risks, you need to add them all up. This is the amount of money you should hold aside for unplanned incidents. It also identifies your most costly risks.

Risk Monetary Value = likelihood of a risk * cost of fixing

Look at your planned activities over the next week or two. If the number of tasks has gone up, you need to get more people and/or spend more money to get the work done. This means you will have to look at your budget.

The money you plan to spend on a task or tasks is the planned value. All the money spent to get you to this point should be assigned to the work already done. This is the actual cost of the work done. If you are seeing results from that work already, you need to keep track of that value.

Earned Value

Use your plan to determine the percentage of completion you have for your task. Once you have this percentage, you can place a dollar amount of the work performed. Your earned value for any effort is the total amount budgeted at the beginning of the project multiplied by the percentage of completion.

Earned Value = Budgeted Cost of Work * % Complete

Performing these simple steps on a regular basis will let you know how you are doing. Identify the impact to your timeline and budget by discovering issues and new risks early. Sometimes you may discover that you need to stop your efforts. If your plans show that your goal is impossible based on the current timeline, budget and resources and they are immoveable; cut your losses. Do not waste your time on an impossible goal. Always rethink and re-plan every chance you get. Plans are not set in stone. They can always be updated and improved. Based on your current point in the project, change or remove tasks.

Listen to your team and look at the numbers. Your support group should be a part of your decision making. Use the advice of your support group to be able to brainstorm your options.

Take a few members of your support team to act as advisors on your project. This is much like a board of directors for a corporation. Guidance from someone who has experience in business is invaluable. New ideas may even get you to your goals faster.

Reworking Plans

Sometimes factors outside your control may require a complete rework of your plans. Be prepared to have a backup plan. Can any current work be reused on a future project? If there is a task that you expect to perform in at least half of every project, consider finding a way to make it easily reusable. You may find there is a need to automate the task or tasks. This may open up new avenues by creating a tool you could resell to others. Whatever you are doing to promote your business is likely to be of value to others.

Return On Investment

Whenever possible, look for completed tasks and products that occur within your project. Whether it is at the end of the project or at the end of a phase, you can show that your efforts have value. The return you get on your invested money, work and energy is an asset to your business.

You can find your return on investment by taking the amount you have earned from an item and divide it by the amount spent to create it. Expressed as a percentage, this is the return on your investment.

As an example, you are making a program that teaches how to build an email list. You spend 16 hours to complete it. The cost of making the program would be your hourly rate, say $50 an hour, times the number of hours. Your product costs $800 to make.

To market it online costs you another $1,200 dollars. Your product has brought in $4,000 dollars. The return on your investment is $4,000 divided by $2,000 or 200%.

Always look at your return on investment, or ROI, to give you a measure of the success of your project.

ROI = amount earned / amount spent * 100%

Look at your Marketing and Online Platforms as well and calculate the return on your marketing investments. For every dollar you spend in advertising you should be able to identify the amount that was returned in sales. This will give you an index to use that identifies your most successful campaigns.

Keep a record of these indicators of your success. Reusing everything that works over time helps you achieve more success by using your budgets and effort wisely.

Split Testing

Your Online Platform should be evaluated for its effectiveness. Internet marketers use a technique called "split testing' to evaluate the effectiveness of different campaigns. Two or more different varieties of presentation and/or pay per click sources are used to see which performs better.

The amount of times an ad is presented is the number of impressions. Using the number of times a customer clicks on your ad, an index of performance can be identified. The click through rate (CTR) is the number of impressions divided by the number of times a person clicks on the ad.

CTR = number of impressions/ number of clicks * 100%

Click through rates vary and depend on the placement of the ad as well as the keywords being used. On the whole, a 2% click through is considered good.

Keeping good records of ads, placement, your search engine position and page design will give you a history related to click through rate. Once you know what your average click through rate is, you can use it to determine your average compared to the general average. If your average is higher, your techniques are working. If they are lower, you may want to consider getting some help.

Unsubscribe Index

If your email list is the key factor in reaching a target audience, then losing someone from your mailing list is a concern. You should create an index of the unsubscribed from your list. Look at the weekly and monthly losses you have.

Take the number of people who unsubscribe and divide it by your total number of subscribers. Taken as a percent, this is your loss of subscriber rate. If you have 1,000 subscribers and 100 unsubscribe in a month, your unsubscribe rate is 10%.

Unsubscribe index = number of unsubscribed accounts / total subscribers

There are other items to track. The number of times an ad is presented (number of impressions) and the number of times it is clicked are important metrics.

In addition, there are bounce rates that track the number of emails that are returned in a campaign. A hard bounce is an email returned as an invalid address. A soft bounce is a returned email for a temporary error identified by the mail server. Reducing any error in your email campaigns is important.

Remember everything online is tracked. Your online reputation is as important as your reputation as a good citizen or good businessperson. Use the information in your plans and your campaign results. Use and reuse these numbers to repeat the most successful campaigns. Know where your campaign is statistically on an ongoing basis.

Chapter 12

YOUR
SUCCESS
PLATFORM

To be able to understand how you are faring as you run your business, it is helpful to have a plan for evaluating your success. There are well documented averages that can be used as guides. The biggest advantage you have today is that almost all the statistics you might want to use are available online.

Business Category

In the United States, every industry has a unique business code that is used at tax time. Find out what category your business is in. Get the current statistics for that industry. Obtain the averages for your industry and others. Look for cases where revenue is falling in an industry. This could indicate a shift in purchasing patterns for that industry. What are the percentages of change year to year for your industry? Is your business growing at that rate? Make your planning decisions using these as guides. For public corporations, the value of the company can be determined by multiplying the number of total shares by the stock price. Stock prices can vary a lot over time. Look for a high, low and average valuation over a set time period.

New businesses take time to become a success. Since less than half of new businesses survive the first two years, finding the causes of these failures tells you what to avoid. Understand overall economic indicators and how they affect your business. Nationwide unemployment or growth/production figures tell a lot about the general factors affecting everyone. Your business may have specific items that will influence your company's bottom line.

Incentives and Rebates

Government incentives or rebate programs may be available in your product niche. Your customer may not be aware of the opportunities. As an example, alternative energy products have rebate programs that subsidize the purchase. States and federal government subsidies offer a percentage of the cost of installing solar or wind energy production systems as tax incentives. Customers will use these savings as one of the factors they use in purchasing these systems.

Remind your customer of anything you are selling that may be deductible from their taxes. In the United States, continuing education and other business expenses are tax deductions. These deductions should be included as a potential price reduction for a product. Remember to suggest they consult a tax expert, as you likely are not legally authorized to provide tax advice.

Buying Decisions

Find the factors your customer uses to make a buying decision. Knowing the objections of your customer helps you prepare for the sale. Determine if there is a need that your customer has. Your success relies on the ability to make your target audience aware of a problem they have and offer a good solution.

Make sure your customer is the problem solver. Unless you are talking to the decision maker, you are simply sharing your knowledge. Unless you are talking to decision makers, you will not succeed. If there are multiple decision makers, you will need to include all of them in your discussions. This is especially true with couples who have a common interest in the financial outcome of any decision. As you show them the solution to the problem, focus on each person. A failure to convince all the people with the authority to make a decision could end up with one person exercising their veto power over the whole decision.

Urgency motivates buyers. Discomfort can spur urgency to purchase. When my wife and I purchased our first home, we received a home warranty for a year. In that year, we had drain blockages that required immediate attention. Nothing says get a plumber like a backed up toilet in a one bathroom house. When the warranty was about to expire, there was an urgency to make sure there was a continuation of the home warranty. The expiration of the warranty and the discomfort of the previous plumbing experience gave me urgency to act. It also prioritized my purchasing decision. The problem you are solving must be sufficiently high on your customer's list to move them to action.

Your solution must be good. References and authority opinions about your solution prevents a customer from seeking other providers. At the worst, it places you in the list of top two or three providers. Be the best and have references. People want to know they are making the best decision possible in their buying decisions.

Benefit Selling

Show your customer the benefits of your solution. Every solution there must have a return on that investment. Show how the customer's investment will have a positive return. I considered putting solar panels on my house. I received multiple quotes and researched the installation and costs. I was unable to find a return on my investment (ROI) within the timeframe I expected. You must find the time frame your customer expects to see a return on their investment. You will also need to know what the return on investment is. If you are not asked about the ROI from your customer, educate them.

If there are commonly accepted business principles related to your solution, you should adhere to them. If you are proposing a new type of solution, make sure you have evidence that your solution works. Use test cases or expert evidence to back up your claims. A commonly accepted and well proven product is easier to sell than something brand new. Even businesses rarely use the latest version of a software product.

Your history will have a lot to say about your customer acceptance. Length of time in business, references and successful implementations are common factors that influence a purchase. If you are new to your business, you may want to joint venture with someone established in your field. Having the approval of an established provider solidifies your reputation to potential customers. Professional references can go a long way to overcome objections.

In a world where there are alternative solutions to a problem, prove that your solution is best. If your solution is well established, you should provide compelling reasons for choosing you as the provider. Case studies and references establish your solution as a proven one. If your solution is new or unique, resolve your customer's objections early.

A new product is not necessarily a bad product. Give your customer compelling reasons to choose your solution.

Lessons Learned

Your Success Platform relies on your successes and failures. It also requires that you document what works and what does not work. Success requires an analysis of each sale. Use your notebook to write down the areas of objection that you have addressed. Every lost sale is an education. You should be able to write down the objection and ways to overcome it.

Your attitude and morale are major factors in your success. Goals and vision are the results of hard work and planning. Addressing all the possibilities that you may encounter prepares you for the issues you may encounter. All of this helps you to have control as you work on your plan.

The Unexpected

There will be times when all the planning in the world cannot predict something that has happened to you. Everything in life goes in cycles. You can choose how you interpret the cycles of your personal and business life. Your attitude towards the world affects everyone. Allow yourself to view the cycles in life from a level center. Understand that for every good time there will be a not so good time. Avoid riding the ups and downs like a roller coaster. This requires a personal review of your actions and attitudes on a regular basis.

Fears versus Fantasies

Assume fears are our negative experiences. Fantasies are our positive desires. Determine if you naturally choose fear or fantasy.

The easier choice for most people is to choose fears. People learn by their experiences. When there is a negative experience, we find it does resolve in time. Our experience shows us that there are other negative experiences we encounter afterward. In time, we learn by experience that there is a wealth of negative experiences available to us. For most people, finding positive experiences is less abundant.

Based on our experience, we begin to expect the negative rather than the positive. Possibly, we are not sure there is a wealth of positive experiences available to us.

Make the choice for positive experiences. Choose fantasy over fear. Have the expectation of the positive experience.

Positive Presentation

Your presentation to the world around you should be a choice you make. I was working as a project manager at a major firm in California. My workload was suddenly doubled with tasks that were not in the original job description. Initially, I was unhappy. I was negative about the job in general for a few days. I realized I was being negative. I decided to look at what was making me unhappy. I made a conscious decision and became pleasant and professional. Over time, the tasks became manageable. In addition, my attitude began to reflect on my coworkers. They expressed their appreciation for my positive attitude and helpfulness.

People like to work with pleasant, helpful people. Be that kind of person. If you are not naturally positive, start your process of change. Put yourself on a six week plan to be pleasant and helpful at every opportunity. When you find you have negative attitudes or thoughts, take inventory of your feelings and expectations. Make a decision. Change direction. Become positive. After six weeks, you will find that your pleasant disposition is a habit.

Five Year Plan

You should have a five year plan based on what you know today. Follow the same techniques in this book and create the detail of what you next five years looks like. If you cannot be sure of the products you will have, list them as a quantity of product types. Have a sales platform for each year of the five years. Make a profit and loss statement for those five years. Estimated sales and expenses can be calculated from your business history. Increase costs and income for each year by the expected inflation.

Include any additional expenses that could occur for you. If you become successful, you may need to hire employees. Employees will require leasing a business space. Your insurance and other costs will increase. Accounting and business consulting costs will increase. Estimate everything. As you continue to succeed at your business, update your five year plan. Put actual values in monthly. Extend your plan by one month each time.

Goals and Change

Everything changes. Your business and plans will change. If this means adding a new business, you will need to use your Success Platforms activities to create new plans for that addition.

Your goals should always stay achievable. Success Platforms is your template to understand what it takes to be successful. It can also help you decide if a goal is worth the effort. You can understand the time, money and effort needed to complete your goal. Your expectations will be balanced against the resources you have. Your positive attitude will be helped by understanding the realities of your plans.

Keep track of the lessons you learn. You can prepare for the unexpected using the lessons learned from your mistakes and others. It is useful to ask others about the lessons they learned and mistakes they made.

Your support group is important. They should be people with similar goals and incomes. It is even better if you have people who are far ahead of you in reaching their goals.

If you are not supported by friends or family, limit your contacts. Keep all negative influences to a minimum. As you become more successful, you will find people approach you differently anyway. They will recognize the success you are achieving. As more people identify with your success, you will find others wanting your time. At this point, your time will also become a commodity. You can charge more for your time and expert opinion.

Your positive approach can be contagious. Infect everyone you know with kindness and positive attitude.

Integrity is a critical element to success. Your integrity is one of the things your customer buys with your product. You may see certain businesses advertise that they have ISO2000 certification. This is a measure of quality that business can use to verify that they have high reliability. In essence the business certifies what they say they do as a business and the certification verifies it. Your mantra for your success should be: "I say what I do and I do what

I say." The quality of your products and your service should be the very best.

Make sure that you are selling what people will buy. Your market research is the best indicator of your success. What you are selling should be in a niche that people spend money. Make sure you provide a product that offers value better than your potential competitors. Shop your competition. Major department stores shop their competitors to understand what the customer sees as advantages in buying from them. Using this information, they can adjust their sales presentation to compete better. Do your market research and use it to your advantage.

You should have your personal brand represented on a website with your name followed by dot com. My personal brand is represented at http://www.bryaneaton.com . Your professional brands will each have their own websites. In my case, the product representing this book and its associated programs is at http://www.successplatforms.com.

You now have the basic tools to climb your Success Platforms. Start using them now. Every day you will build on each step you have made previously. Over time, small steps build massive platforms. Each one will help you succeed.

SUCCESS PLATFORMS RESOURCES

Training Programs

Do you want to discover the platforms that lead to success and your business improvement? Our **Success Platforms Training Programs** are specifically designed to reach your business goals.

Our team of experts will help you build the platforms for your success with entertaining, fun and informative seminars. You and your team will walk away with a structured platform to:

- Increase your productivity levels,
- Develop improvements in communications internally and externally,
- Improve your productivity in measurable ways,
- Significantly improve your company's teamwork and alliance to common goals

And much more.

Visit our website at http://www.SuccessPlatforms.com to learn more about how we can help you and your team build the Success Platforms that improve your business goals.

BOOK BRYAN EATON TO SPEAK AT YOUR NEXT EVENT

After more than 20 years of creating success for people in small and large businesses, Bryan Eaton has discovered that Success is simple, when you know the steps to get you there. The thing is, building and growing a business requires more than just putting a product out there and waiting for people to want it. The sad truth is only half of all new businesses survive more than 2 years.

As an award winning Music Director at NBC radio, and certified Project Manager in Fortune 500 companies, Bryan Eaton has seen all the short cuts that work and the ones that don't.

Meeting planners can count on Bryan Eaton to provide keynotes that entertain and inform. Bryan's unique background in transformational change in businesses makes him unique. He's been in the trenches using the simple strategies that make the difference in business today and tomorrow. Using these strategies he has transformed products into multi-million dollar businesses. Bryan has personally helped companies like NBC,

IBM, Symantec, Verizon, and others get their projects done using these processes.

The fact is, it's not hard at all, once you know the right systems to make Success Platforms into a business no-brainer. Bryan believes everyone deserves success, and as an author, speaker and coach, it is his goal to make sure every entrepreneur and small business owner gets a chance to know the excitement of making their business soar.

Contact Bryan and let's discuss how your team can see that business is not so hard at all with the right formulas for success. Bryan can show your team that it's okay for people to make their passion their success. Let Bryan show the simple processes that anyone can use to consistently produce a winning outcome in business.

ABOUT THE AUTHOR

 Bryan Eaton started his professional career in radio and television broadcasting, transitioned to computers systems development and then a certified Project Management Professional. Mr. Eaton was a Music Director and Assistant Program Manager at the NBC radio outlet in San Francisco where they were awarded Billboard magazine's Station of the Year. Bryan also was a radio announcer in Las Vegas, Nevada and Monterey, California. Mr. Eaton also worked as a business conference audio visual professional. Bryan was co-host and producer for segments of the March of Dimes telethon in Las Vegas. He also served on the Board of Directors for the Las Vegas chapter of the March of Dimes.

Mr. Eaton was a research subject for the best-selling book Fit or Fat by Covert Bailey. In the late 1980s, Bryan created the first multimedia baseball card. Bryan is also a historian who created the first collection of color Abraham Lincoln photos. His first book, Color of Lincoln, provided the first comprehensive updated colorization of the collection of photographs of Abraham Lincoln. The photos and full color book are part of the Lincoln Collection at the Abraham Presidential Library in Springfield, Illinois.

Mr. Eaton has held his PMP, project management certification since 2005. As a project management consultant, Bryan has successfully managed multi-million dollar projects in disciplines from broadcasting to healthcare. He lives in the San Francisco bay area with his wife, Natalie.

FORMULAS

Please, scan the code below to access the formulas and relevant reference material online.

INDEX